BRODICK-ARRAN AND THE GREAT WAR, 1914-1918

A

BRODICK—ARRAN
AND THE GREAT WAR
1914-1918

BY

JAMES C. INGLIS

OLIVER AND BOYD
EDINBURGH: TWEEDDALE COURT
LONDON: 33 PATERNOSTER ROW, E.C.

1919

Printed and bound by Antony Rowe Ltd, Eastbourne

DEDICATED TO

THE GALLANT LADS

AND TO

THE MEMORY OF

"THE UNRETURNING BRAVE"

Preface

WHILE the impressions of the Great War are still fresh in the memories of those who have lived through the eventful time, it seems fitting that some permanent record should be made of these impressions.

It is also due to the memory of the men who have gone through the great ordeal, to preserve a record of their services, particularly of those who have made the supreme sacrifice—" They went forth to the battle and never came back."

Knowing the greater number of the lads personally, this compilation has been a work of pleasure; but I regret that in all cases I did not succeed in obtaining as many particulars as I would have liked, so that where details are somewhat meagre, it is not due to lack of effort.

THE AUTHOR.

INVERCLOY, BRODICK,
29th March 1919.

BRODICK-ARRAN AND THE GREAT WAR, 1914-1918

Introduction

THE summer of 1914 will be ever memorable in the annals of history. It was a fateful time for Europe, for the whole world. The dark clouds looming on the horizon, which burst with awful fury and started a conflagration the like of which the world had never seen, with consequences so widespread and appalling, were eagerly watched, and the matter discussed with a gravity befitting the time. To those with a knowledge of the general situation it was evident that Great Britain would become involved, not only from the point of view of the safety of the Empire, but having plighted her word to safeguard the neutrality and independence of Belgium, it would have been dishonourable to her honoured name to have stood idly by. The British Cabinet had a momentous question to decide, but our statesmen being men of honour and integrity, knowing well the awful consequences that were bound up in the question, faced the matter with equanimity and decided to enter the conflict on behalf of maintaining the freedom of this

Brodick-Arran and the Great War

free-loving country and of mankind generally, a decision in which the whole British Empire freely acquiesced.

Coming at a time when Arran was full of visitors, that decision caused tremendous excitement, and on that ever memorable day in the beginning of August when the decision became known, and for successive days, nothing was talked of but the war— the war was on everybody's lips. Posters were exhibited calling men to the Colours, and several residing temporarily on the Island were off with all speed to join their respective units. The inhabitants, from the oldest to the youngest, were on the alert to hear the latest. The holding up of the German legions at Liège by the heroic Belgians gave much satisfaction, and the dispatching of the Expeditionary Force from Britain gave room for great speculation, as no details were published in the Press. However, the meagre details that filtered through about "the contemptible little army" encountering the enemy at Mons, and the fighting retreat that followed, only whetted the appetite of the public, setting everybody on the *qui vive* for the latest news. Newspapers were eagerly bought up, and the people in some of the districts were informed of the latest particulars by wire from the *Glasgow Herald* each afternoon or evening.

Many stories, arising in the minds of imaginative people, got into circulation throughout the country, one of these being the Russian myth. Frequently one heard it positively asserted that train-loads of

Introduction

Russians were passing through Scotland on their way to France, where they would help to stay the German advance. So positively and, in some cases, so convincingly was this assertion made, that one was almost persuaded to believe it. However, as time wore on, the story was completely discredited. One explanation of its origin, it was said, had arisen from the fact that as a train-load of Highlanders were passing through a certain railway station they were asked from whence they came, and the answer came back "from Ross-shire," in tones that seemed to sound like "from Russia." Be that as it may, it came to be known conclusively that not a Russian had set foot in France until long afterwards.

As time slipped past and the dark gloomy days of winter wore on, the facilities for obtaining news became limited, newspapers being only received by the forenoon steamer. Consequently, by next morning we might be far in arrears of what was happening. That being so, many of the inhabitants of Brodick, and I believe in other districts also, subscribed to a fund which enabled them to get the latest particulars by wire each evening from the *Glasgow Herald* throughout the winter months. Needless to say, the interest was great, as testified by the number who congregated at Brodick Post Office nightly, and if not thoroughly satisfied with the progress of events, they were nevertheless pleased that our forces kept the enemy at bay, preventing them from breaking through to Calais.

Patriotism had risen to a high level. The war had

Brodick-Arran and the Great War

not long begun when many of the young men in Brodick and other districts gallantly volunteered their services to King and country, and as they left from time to time the steamer invariably sounded a long farewell on her siren as she swung off from the various piers.

The authorities were on the alert. Very soon after war was declared, Government representatives visited the Island and commandeered all the available horses they could lay hands on, giving a good price, however, to the owners, and somewhere about eighty were obtained. The first batch were lifted on the forenoon of Sabbath the 9th August by the Caledonian steamer *Duchess of Argyle*, and conveyed to Rothesay. It was a unique sight indeed for the inhabitants, in strange contrast to the usual quiet state of that day, to see horses being conveyed to the piers. It gave one the impression of a market day, and still there was something strange; there was an absence of the usual stir and turmoil of everyday life, with a serenity pervading the atmosphere, denoting, after all, that it was the Sabbath. Curiosity attracted many to witness the embarkation, and as an old man mingled with the throng on his way to Brodick Pier, he had doubtless vivid recollections of the old-time Sabbath of his youth, as he gave vent to the following expression in subdued tones: "This is not like the Sabbaths we have been accustomed to in Arran."

With all the patriotism of the Arran youths, their ardour was severely damped by a ridiculous

Introduction

paragraph in a Glasgow evening paper, that all that Arran had contributed in the early days to the fighting forces was eighty horses and one man, a statement which naturally brought about a good deal of resentment.

But even if that were the case, Arran was at a great disadvantage in comparison with many other places. There were no trained men on the Island. The Territorials had never been established—due to what, one may well ask; certainly not to the apathy of the young men of the eastern side of the Island, at anyrate, for in the year 1881 an attempt was made by those in Brodick, Lamlash, and Corrie to have a Volunteer corps established, but the movement, which was on the fair way to success, had to be abandoned for the want of accommodation for drilling and shooting.

Had the movement received the support necessary to carry it through, Arran men at the outbreak of hostilities would have been able to take their places alongside of their comrades on the mainland, and if there were not many Arran men in the early stages of the fighting, it is not that they were indifferent; but, after all, Arran was not unrepresented even in these days, for many of her sons who were out in the world had the necessary training which enabled them to take their part in the early stages of the struggle.

From personal observation and close contact with the people of Brodick, of which district I go on now to speak about more particularly, a fine spirit was manifest among the lads, and from what I have

Brodick-Arran and the Great War

heard, an equally fine spirit was also manifest in other districts, so much so that I verily believe, had there been one then to lead and organise them, a good contingent might have been earlier in the field; but while saying this, I don't forget that the Marquis of Graham endeavoured to obtain recruits for the Navy; however, this branch of the service did not appeal to them, although at a later date quite a number found their way there. Meanwhile the youths were gradually going away; there was an impulse carrying them along which they could not resist; they had heard their country's call, their country was in danger, but no foreign invader would reach the shores of Britain if they could help to stem the onrush on the stricken fields of France and Belgium. No, the freedom for which their forefathers bled and died was not to be filched away by this proud and unscrupulous usurper. As I look back over those four years of terrible suffering and cruelty, my thoughts go out to these brave fellows, some of whom I saw going off in the early days. They were objects of special interest as they passed along to the embarking stage with a firm and buoyant stride. The thoughts of the populace went after them, and they wondered—yes, many of them wondered—what would befall them. Would they ever come back? Well, some of them have come back, wounded and crippled in body, while others lie mouldering on the battle-fields of France—the battles of Loos and the Somme were fateful days for them—and some have come through it all.

Introduction

As I have said, the youths were gradually going away, some of them encouraged by the presence of recruiting officers, who made a detour of the Island; and in December 1915, when the Derby Scheme came into operation, all the remaining eligible youths in Brodick attested. Some failed to pass the test; nevertheless, it was gratifying that they had offered themselves, and those who did pass were called up by the authorities as required. Later, as young men came of military age, after the Military Act came into operation, they did not like the idea of being called conscripts—no, the very name was repugnant to their natures, and they invariably attested voluntarily before being called to the Colours. Ultimately, the district became completely denuded of young men, with the exception of a few exempted by the County Tribunal and those unfit for military service.

This description of the state of things in Brodick may be equally applied to the villages throughout the Island where they were unhampered by agricultural pursuits, and in a varying degree generally.

At the national registration in August 1915, it was computed that there were 1000 males in Arran between fifteen and sixty-five years of age, and I am told Arran has contributed 500 men to the fighting forces since the beginning of the war. That being so, if the number above military age is taken into consideration, and those exempted for agriculture and other purposes, it is apparent she has given a good quota.

Brodick-Arran and the Great War

Arran men, sons of Arran men, and descendants of Arran men, are to be found in all branches of the service, and serving in all parts of the war zone. Besides those who have gone direct from Arran, many have come from all parts of the Empire—from Canada and the rolling plains of the West, as well as from the great sheep-walks of Australasia and the mining camps of South Africa. Some who went "down to the sea in ships" have had the trying experience of having been submarined, and the bodies of the less fortunate are now "where pearls lie deep"; others have come through engagements in the Navy; while others again lie buried in the Eastern and Western fronts. Some have returned to their respective lands disabled and discharged, and while gradual demobilisation is proceeding, a number are still with their units, some of them now on duty beyond the Rhine.

Many from across the seas have revisited their old homes and parents in Arran, and many more have made the pilgrimage to see their friends in the land of their forefathers, which in bygone days they had heard of and dreamt much about. Fine, gallant fellows they were, good specimens of Colonial humanity. As a typical example, I may say that I had the pleasure recently of meeting a Canadian in Brodick from the Bay of Chaleur. His grandfather had left the Island wellnigh a century ago. He, however, did not know from what part of Arran he had gone, but he had come to see "the lovely Island," with the hope that he might come across some

Introduction

relatives. He spoke of the early settlers in the Bay of Chaleur from Arran and other parts of Scotland, recounting the hardships they had to endure. "They were heroes," he said, "just as much so as those brave fellows who were 'going over the top' in this great war." Complimented on the good work of the Canadian soldiers, he drew a long breath and exclaimed, "Ah, it is because they are Scotch!" And in this expression one can easily discern the attachment and love for the old land.

The effects of the war on the general life of Arran have been very apparent. From the commencement of the struggle changes became manifest, due to the general regulations of D.O.R.A. With the gradual depletion of young men the usual animation of village life frittered away, and the resulting quietness intensified by the strict enforcement of the general order regarding the obscuring of lights visible from the sea, and, later, to all lights when the Zepps began their nocturnal raids. Under these conditions it seemed so strange as one ventured out of doors into utter darkness, especially in the long winter nights, not a gleam of light being seen in the glens and villages—nothing but the stars overhead on a clear night, with the occasional flash of the lighthouses in the distance.

To guard further against an enemy surprise night watchmen were appointed to patrol the Island, and in the districts of Brodick and Lamlash particularly a system of voluntary night patrolling was established, when about a dozen of the residents were told off in couples to take two shifts each per week; but this after a time, however, was only carried out when danger was supposed to be lurking about. Alert while on duty, a mysterious light was observed by the watchmen on the hillside above Brodick Castle, which from its blinking tendency conveyed the impression that probably some one was conniving with the enemy. After an "eerie" walk the mystery was still unsolved, but eventually it was discovered to be caused by the action of the wind fanning the embers of an old tree-stump on which rubbish had been burned previously. The showing of lights or fires at night was in some cases very seriously dealt with. Unfortunately, several farmers throughout the Island were heavily fined for neglecting to extinguish fires on the hillsides after the burning of heather during the day.

In the spring of 1915 there was a scare in the firth of enemy submarines having been about, indeed it is possible they were not far away. In consequence, many stories originated, and as they passed from mouth to mouth they became so exaggerated that one was almost persuaded to believe that the seas about the shores of Arran were infested with these pirates. So much were the public under the impression that it was really dangerous to make the voyage from Ardrossan to Arran, that house-letting at the beginning of the season was at a very low ebb, and consequently those depending on this source of income for their livelihood were very much crippled—indeed, Arran as a whole felt the effects seriously.

Introduction

However, the scare gradually wore off and the confidence of travellers restored, so that by midsummer Brodick and the other resorts were comparatively busy again.

After this recovery these conditions were very much maintained until the spring of 1917, when another scare was announced, which had also a very bad effect, even worse than the last, for many who had houses taken for the summer months cancelled them; and one cannot be surprised, for this scare was one in reality—submarines were undoubtedly about. Ships were held up in Lamlash by our own authorities for safety, as well as on other parts of the firth. The night watchmen were now on the alert, and, due to the vigilance of the man at Corrie, a noise resembling that of a submarine was heard by him one very quiet night in the direction of the Garroch-Head, which was at once reported to the proper quarter; and it was currently stated, indeed it was generally believed as certain, that our vigilant Navy was soon in these waters and caught one laying mines, which they destroyed.

For his vigilance, Thomas Kelso, the Corrie watchman, was subsequently presented with a cheque for £25 by the Admiralty.

Not many nights afterwards, as William Davidson was patrolling round Brodick Bay on a very still, quiet night, with not a ripple on the water, and just such a night when the least sound could be easily detected, he distinctly heard, when in the vicinity of the old pier below the castle, sounds, very distinct sounds, resembling the dropping of an anchor somewhere off Corriegills. Convinced that there was something unusual happening, he reported his suspicions to the head of the watchmen, George Laidler, factor, Strabane, and he in turn to headquarters. Mr Laidler's position, I may here say, as organiser and head of the Arran Coast watchers, was entirely honorary. Whether it was actually the result of this report I am not in a position to say, but on the following morning mine-sweepers were successful in discovering mines which it would appear had been laid to catch the shipping going up and down the channel, but more possibly into Lamlash. About ten o'clock that morning a loud explosion was distinctly heard which was believed to be due to the explosion of a mine.

Meanwhile the *Glensannox* was making the forenoon run from Ardrossan and getting well on to the entrance to Brodick Bay, when one of the mine-sweepers approached and warned the captain that he was running into danger, and directed him to miss Brodick and follow into Lamlash. People on shore, seeing the sudden change of course, concluded there was something wrong, and naturally there was much consternation and speculation, which was soon cleared up by the arrival of the mails in Brodick by motor car, the passengers making their way thither as best they could. Conversing with one afterwards, he said they passed through a lot of dead fish floating on the surface of the water, due doubtless to the explosion referred to.

Introduction

The steamer lay at Lamlash or Whiting Bay until the following afternoon, when she sailed from these ports for Ardrossan, taking a southerly course to the mainland and striking along the Ayrshire coast. The passage was made on the usual course via Brodick the following day, but for many days afterwards it was made under an Admiralty course via Whiting Bay and skirting close inshore on the way round to Brodick, but eventually got on to the old course via Brodick, much to the relief of the general public. Later an Admiralty course was set striking and departing from the Arran shore at the northern entrance to Lamlash, which constantly received the careful attention of the mine-sweepers, and on which the steamer continued until after the signing of the Armistice. This interruption of traffic had now become serious. For two whole days on the previous week there was no communication whatever with Ardrossan, but on the evening of the third day the *Glensannox* was allowed to make the passage. However, earlier in the day, before the embargo had been lifted, a patrol boat brought across mails, newspapers, and a few passengers who were brave enough to risk the crossing. There were indications that the scare was wearing off. People were beginning again to seek summer quarters; but on Tuesday afternoon of 22nd May, as the *Glensannox* was approaching Ardrossan, she was intercepted by a torpedo-destroyer a few miles from the harbour warning her of the danger ahead, a patrol boat having been blown up shortly before. She was promptly put about and

Brodick-Arran and the Great War

steered for Brodick, where the passengers embarked at Brodick were landed, and then she proceeded to Lamlash and Whiting Bay with the others. Many of those landed at Brodick assembled at the pier next morning in the hope that the steamer might make a morning run, but that did not turn out to be the case, and for the next few days isolation and irregularity were experienced. By the end of the month, however, things had reverted to their normal conditions, and with the exception of a slight interruption towards the end of June, continued until about Christmas and the New Year, after which communication with Arran was free from disturbance.

Nothing unusual having happened down through the spring of 1918, the confidence of the public was fully restored, with the result that by midsummer, notwithstanding a limited railway and steamer service, Arran was full of visitors and quite like itself again, but there was the want of the usual bustle and excitement of pre-war days. The fine palatial steamers that were constantly churning the waters of the firth, running excursions and plying frequently between Arran and the mainland, had been taken over by the Government and employed carrying troops to France and sweeping mines around the coasts. In consequence travelling facilities were gradually reduced until for the last two seasons there was only a connection with Ardrossan once daily, with the exception of Friday and Saturday during July and August, when there was an evening connection as

Introduction

well. The connection from Greenock and Gourock was entirely suspended, as well as the service by the turbine steamer to Lochranza and the west side of the Island, while limited facilities were continued by the old Campbeltown Company to Lochranza and Pirnmill.

The prices of provisions and other commodities had become abnormally high—for example, the 4-lb. loaf had risen to 1s. 1d.; but bread, being the staple article of diet of a vast multitude, the Government, in order to prevent a great hardship, wisely subsidised the trade, and the 4-lb. loaf was put on the market at the maximum price of 9d., with permission, however, to local committees in outlying districts to allow retailers a little extra for the cost of transit; so that in Arran it was procurable at a price ranging from 9d. to 10d., at least that was the case in Brodick, and the bread obtained there was of a quality of whiteness equal to the best that could be procured anywhere. To prevent profiteering, the prices of other merchandise, such as butter, eggs, butcher meat, etc., were also controlled. Although prices had become so inflated, the effects of the war were not seriously felt until the expansion of submarine activity in the spring of 1917, with its consequent destruction of shipping. Farmers were receiving enhanced prices for their produce and surplus stock, merchants for their commodities. Wages had risen in consequence of the high prices prevailing, and the people who really felt the pinch were those wholly dependent on the letting of their houses to visitors, as rents had decreased considerably

Brodick-Arran and the Great War

in conformity with the law of supply and demand, but after all there were no extreme cases of hardship so far as known. In order to cope successfully with these sea pirates, a convoy system was in full swing by the month of August, and it was a unique and interesting sight to see a long line of steamers leaving Lamlash periodically with an escort. The question of conserving tonnage for the transit of troops and war material, which was now required to a much greater degree by the entrance of America into the struggle, had now become so important that imports not really essential for food were cut down to a minimum. The food problem being now acute, especially in the large cities and towns, a system of general rationing had to be resorted to, and by the spring of 1918, sugar, butter, butcher meat, etc., could not be obtained without the necessary coupons, a procedure which distributed food equally among all classes. Unfortunately, as a result of calling up for military service the only butcher left to supply Brodick and surrounding district with butcher meat, a great inconvenience and hardship was experienced for several months by visitors and natives alike, but through representations made to the departments concerned, the situation was relieved by the authorities releasing him from the Army.

On the initiative of the Marchioness of Graham, a branch of the Red Cross Society had been early established on the Island, with a central committee and local committees in every district. Money was collected from time to time and freely given.

Introduction

Towards the end of 1915 an Isle of Arran bed was established and endowed in the Rouen Military Hospital, and the first patient to occupy the bed was Private H. T. Milner, 2nd Battalion Queen's Royal West Surrey Regiment, very appropriately under the care of Sister M'Kinnon, daughter of Peter M'Kinnon, Torrlinn, Arran. Work-parties were organised throughout the Island, and large consignments of garments dispatched to the Red Cross centre in Glasgow, under the supervision of Mrs Laidler, who received letters of thanks, which appeared in the Press from time to time, for the most excellent work sent in by the Arran workers.

Free gift sales were held in aid of the Red Cross funds, which were patronised freely by both visitors and natives, one at Brodick Castle realising about £400, while others at Lamlash, under the auspices of the Arran Food Production Committee and the Arran Farmers Society, realised over £600 each. Besides work done for the Red Cross, funds were raised in every district by concerts and otherwise, to which visitors generously gave their services, to provide comforts for local lads on service, and many of the inhabitants gave private gifts to soldiers generally as well. In all these things the school children, under the guidance of the teachers, took a leading hand, and I have no hesitation in saying that the people of Arran can look back with satisfaction on the part they had in furthering all branches of war work. Those on the various committees in connection with rationing and other war problems did their best in giving effect to the regulations in as fair and generous a way as circumstances permitted, under varying difficulties, and the Food Production Committee particularly has reason to be satisfied with the response to the appeal for more production.

Farmers and plot-holders rose nobly to the occasion, and several hundred more acres were brought under cultivation, but much of the crop of 1918 was wasted in consequence of the weather conditions. Not only did women render valuable assistance in the production of extra food from the land and fill many of the places vacated by men as well, but Arran women were also engaged throughout Great Britain and, at least in some of the war areas, in the more humane work of alleviating the sufferings of the wounded in hospitals, one of the most distinguished being Sister Elizabeth Kerr, Sannox, mentioned in Lord French's dispatches in January 1916, and awarded the R.R.C. (1st class) in January 1917. To this much needed work the Marchioness of Graham applied herself, having been qualified as a Red Cross nurse, and for a time engaged in Bellahouston Hospital, Glasgow, afterwards as Commandant of the Auxiliary Red Cross Hospital for convalescent soldiers established, on her initiative, in the naval canteen at Lamlash in the spring of 1917, in which several local ladies rendered valuable aid. With wounded soldiers moving freely about, patrol boats going out and in the bay, warships coming and going, on some of which the American flag was frequently seen floating in the breeze, and the assembling

Introduction

of the merchant steamers for the convoy, Lamlash had quite an animated and warlike appearance.

During these fateful four years, with the enemy's cruelties, barbarities, and hideous crimes, which can never be effaced from the records of time, the people of Arran, through all the varying vicissitudes of the colossal struggle, never gave way to panic on the one hand nor to undue ecstasy on the other, but to say that there was no depression or anxiety would be a perversion of the truth. At the same time there was a confidence in our leaders and our men, and, above all, in the righteousness of our cause, that however long and hard the path might be, Britain and her allies would ultimately gain the victory. In the intervening time between the presentation of the terms of the Armistice and the signing, the populace keenly discussed the situation and awaited the outcome with eagerness. When it became known on the forenoon of 11th November that the enemy delegates had accepted its terms and signed the historical document, general satisfaction was expressed that right had at last triumphed over might and the struggle had ended. Restraint and anxiety had now been dispelled and a spirit of rejoicing prevailed. While some gave vent to their feelings in levity and the dance, thanksgiving services were also held to which many resorted with grateful hearts.

I now go on to enumerate those belonging to Brodick and connected therewith engaged on active service, including those in the nursing profession, with whom I begin.

Brodick-Arran and the Great War

Nurses

MARY, DUCHESS OF HAMILTON, whose connection with Brodick dates back for nearly half a century, was Commandant of the Easton Park Red Cross Hospital from 29th September 1914 to 14th January 1919, and assiduously attended to her duties, not having left the hospital on more than two brief occasions for rest and recuperation.

THE MARCHIONESS OF GRAHAM, O.B.E., at the outbreak of war undertook Red Cross nursing in her Easton Park residence, which was converted into an Auxiliary Red Cross Hospital. After two years' duty there, she went to Bellahouston Red Cross Hospital to undertake further duties, and remained there for about six months. Owing to there being a call for further Red Cross Auxiliary Hospitals, the naval canteen at Lamlash, as already stated, was converted into one in April 1917, and the Marchioness, as Commandant, took up residence in the Whitehouse, Lamlash, where the nursing staff was also accommodated.

In recognition of her services she was decorated in June 1918 with the insignia of the Order of the British Empire.

Mrs ZURCHER, eldest daughter of James Kelso, Alma Terrace, who was formerly a fully qualified nurse in London, nursed in the South African War

Nurses

from the time Lord Roberts took over the command. Mentioned in despatches by Lord Roberts, she also received the Queen Victoria War Medal. Settling in South Africa, she afterwards got charge of the European Hospital in Zanzibar, in which many of those on active service in that region in the present war were nursed, including men from both the Army and Navy. For her good work there she has received the honour of the Royal Red Cross, and a letter of thanks from the Admiral in Command of the African Squadron.

Sister CATHERINE STEWART, fourth daughter of the late John Stewart, Invercloy, was for three years in the M'Alpine Home, Glasgow, where she was taught everything relating to private nursing. She afterwards entered King's College Hospital, London, for general training, and qualifying there as a fully-trained nurse, immediately joined the Territorial Nursing Force as a nursing sister. King's College having been turned into a Military Hospital, she was given a post there, and many of our gallant lads passed through her hands. She was on the list for foreign service, but prevented twice from going as she could not be spared from her present duties.

Sister BESSIE M'NICOL, Queen Alexandra Imperial Military Nursing Reserve, daughter of the late Alexander M'Nicol, Corriegills, was trained in Glasgow Western Infirmary, and later in a Military Hospital, Newcastle; went to Salonica early in 1918,

Brodick-Arran and the Great War

where she has charge of twenty-one marquees, with twenty-nine beds in each. She is fully trained.

Nurse ROGERS, Brodick District Nurse, has been employed periodically nursing in Easton Park and Lamlash Auxiliary Hospitals.

Mrs GUTHRIE, elder daughter of Dugald Langlands, Invercloy, nursed in Kirklandside Hospital, Kilmarnock, and later in Northumberland War Hospital, Newcastle-on-Tyne.

Royal Navy

THE MARQUIS OF GRAHAM, C.B., C.V.O., Captain R.N.V.R., Divisional Coast Watch Officer for the South-west of Scotland, was mobilised with the R.N.V.R. at the outbreak of war on 2nd August 1914 with the rank of Commander, and he successfully undertook the recruiting in Scotland for the Naval Division, for which thousands of recruits were obtained. He also devoted his attention to the organisation of the Coast Watch Service; was appointed Captain R.N.V.R. in 1916, D.C.W.O. in 1917 for the South-west of Scotland, and was Competent Naval Authority, under D.O.R.A., for Glasgow and Clyde area. The drifters *Bon Ami*, *Pass-Away*, and *Lustre Gem*, also the yachts *Mairi*, *Branwen*, and *Gael*, were under his command. He was demobilised on 21st January 1919, and has

Royal Navy

always taken a keen interest in the Navy, especially in the R.N.V.R. branch of it.

P. A. MURCHIE, Lieutenant-Commander R.N.R., son-in-law of Alexander Wooley, Invercloy, was an officer on board the S.S. *Carmania*, of the Cunard Company of Liverpool, when war broke out, and a Lieutenant in the Royal Naval Reserve. The *Carmania* having been taken over by the Admiralty as an auxiliary cruiser, he was on 8th August 1914 appointed Lieutenant R.N.R. on this vessel, which proceeded to the south-east coast of America, and was engaged in operations against raiders, under Rear-Admiral Sir C. Craddock. Falling in with the enemy auxiliary cruiser *Cap Trafalgar* on 13th September, the German ship was sunk by the *Carmania* after a stiff engagement. Appointed to succeed Commander J. C. Barr, C.B., R.N.R., as Navigating Officer of the *Carmania* on 12th November 1914, he served on the Atlantic Station under Rear-Admiral Sir Arthur Moore, K.C.B., from December 1914 to April 1915, and was subsequently engaged in the Dardanelles Expedition during May and June. After refitting at Devonport, he served on mid-Atlantic patrol, off the Canaries and Madeira, and was later in temporary command of the Austrian prize *Karpat*, captured at sea. He also served as Navigating Lieutenant of H.M.S. *Leander*, and as Lieutenant R.N.R. on H.M.S. *Fisgard*. For a considerable time he was in command of H.M.S. *Grangemouth*, employed in anti-submarine duties in

Brodick-Arran and the Great War

the Mediterranean; on 31st December 1917 promoted to Lieutenant-Commander for meritorious service at sea; and in July following appointed Navigating Lieutenant-Commander on H.M.S. *Tyne*, parent ship of the 8th Destroyer Flotilla. Was demobilised in January 1919.

JOHN FULLARTON, Surgeon-Commander, only son of Captain Duncan Fullarton, late of the Mercantile Marine, and nephew of the Misses Fullarton, Rosebank, Invercloy, was a surgeon in the Navy previous to the war. Born in Glasgow, he was brought up with his grandparents in Brodick, and received his early education in Brodick and Lamlash schools, afterwards at Ayr Academy, and later at Edinburgh University, where he graduated. He was on duty on H.M.S. *Patrol*, which was badly damaged in an engagement with the enemy at the bombardment of Scarborough in December 1914. Subsequently he was Staff Surgeon on the battleship *Glory*, on duty in the Far North, and promoted to Surgeon-Commander after his return from northern waters in the summer of 1918.

WILLIAM BROWN, Warrant Officer (1st Class), son-in-law of William Walker, Invercloy, enlisted in the Royal Marine Light Infantry, at Glasgow, on 24th June 1901. During his career he has served on various ships—viz., *Cambridge*, 1902; *Hood*, 1903; *Empress of India*, 1904-5; *Hannibal*, 1906-8; *Suffolk*, 1910-12.

Royal Navy

In this war Royal Marines have been serving on every front and on almost every ship of the Navy, as well as gunners in the Mercantile Marine. With great gallantry a battalion stormed the Zeebrugge Mole on St George's Day of last year, and had 70 per cent. casualties. Since 1915 this corps has been greatly strengthened, and records of their deeds might be multiplied. They have served in almost every campaign since 1664, and in this war of wars have upheld their reputation and gained every distinction, from the V.C. downwards, on both land and sea.

At the outbreak of war the subject of this sketch was serving at Plymouth, and shortly after was embarked on H.M.S. *Marlborough*, one of the ships of the Grand Fleet, on which he went through the battle of Jutland serving as one of the crew of a 13·9 gun. Their shooting was reported on as excellent, and they were credited with doing a lot of damage; but they, however, did not get off "scot free," being hit with a "tin fish" and having trouble to reach port.

He disembarked in April 1917 for special work on the General Staff of Royal Marines at the Admiralty, where he is now serving. While afloat he held the rank of sergeant, but since coming ashore has reached the height of warrant officer, 1st class.

ARCHIBALD CURRIE, Engine-Room Artificer, R.N.R., Greenock, eldest son of the late Archibald Currie, Douglas Row, was mobilised on 2nd August 1914, and proceeded next day to Portsmouth Naval

Brodick-Arran and the Great War

Depot. A week later he was sent on board the auxiliary cruiser *Armadale Castle* of the Union Castle Line, then fitting out at Southampton, which was later engaged patrolling the African coast, particularly in German South-west, where they destroyed a wireless station that had been giving trouble.

Having been invalided in October to the R.N. Hospital at Simon's Town, from which he was removed to England at the end of February and admitted to Haslar Hospital, Gosport, he was finally discharged medically unfit about the middle of April 1915.

That closed his brief career in the war so far as active service was concerned, but on recovery he entered the torpedo factory at Greenock.

JAMES HALLIDAY, Engineer-Lieutenant R.N.R., third son of the late William Halliday at one time head gamekeeper at Brodick Castle, entered Government service early in the war, the steamer *Brighton Queen*, on which he was then serving, having been taken over by the Admiralty. For some time on this vessel, mine-sweeping in the North Sea, he was later on the *Barry*, the last transport to leave Suvla Bay at the evacuation of the peninsula, being afterwards transferred to the P.S. *Jupiter* of the Glasgow and South-Western Railway Company, in Government service in the Western war zone.

HUGH DEWAR, eldest son of the late John Dewar (second marriage) head gamekeeper at Brodick

Royal Navy

Castle, joined the Hawke Battalion Royal Naval Volunteers in October 1914, landed at Gallipoli in April 1915, was wounded twice and lost the sight of an eye, took enteric fever and was nursed at the Naval Hospital, Malta, later in the Naval Hospital, Greenwich, and since recovery has been on duty at the Crystal Palace, London.

ALEXANDER M'KELVIE, a local coal agent, eldest son of the late Andrew M'Kelvie, Corriegills, enlisted in December 1915, and was a stoker on the auxiliary cruiser *Hildebrand* continuously since, patrolling the seas and engaged on convoy duty from American and African ports. Fortunately, on account of his vessel being delayed through assisting a disabled ship, he escaped being in the great disaster in Halifax harbour. Was demobilised in January 1919.

ROBERT ROBERTSON, employed about the Douglas Hotel Farm, also joined the *Hildebrand* about the same time as M'Kelvie, and became a greaser on that vessel.

PETER S. LANGLANDS, Gunner, an apprentice baker with Messrs A. Wooley & Son, Brodick, younger son of Dugald Langlands, Invercloy, joined the Lovat Scouts in November 1915, but his employer had him exempted. In March 1916, however, he joined the Navy, and after the usual training at Devonport was appointed a gunner on the merchant steamer *Pendarves*, and acted successively in the

Brodick-Arran and the Great War

same capacity on the *Nailsea Court*, *Holthom Newton*, *Carib Prince*, and the schooner *Katie*, sailing between Runcorn and Cornwall, also on the P. & O. Liner *Poona*. The *Nailsea Court* was unfortunately submarined off the south-west of Ireland, on a voyage from Philadelphia, but Peter and his mate stood gallantly by their gun until they had to leap overboard as the ship settled down, and were rescued by the crew, who had previously taken to the boats, and ultimately picked up by a cruiser which appeared on the scene. The captain reported their gallant conduct to the Admiralty.

The *Holthom Newton* was also attacked by a submarine off the Irish coast, but escaped without damage, the gunners having compelled the enemy craft to submerge. Their dangers, however, were not yet over. Off Dover they were shelled by four enemy destroyers, but again escaped safely.

ROBERT HENDRY, A.B., eldest son of David Hendry, Low Glencloy, was an employee in Brodick Post Office and enlisted in January 1916. Trained at the Royal Naval Barracks, Devonport, he was drafted to H.M.S. *Lizard* (torpedo-destroyer), and after a fortnight's experience at sea was in action at the battle of Jutland, afterwards doing convoy duties in the Irish Channel, where the *Lizard* had the misfortune to collide with another destroyer while steaming with lights out. On rejoining his ship after the necessary repairs, they were for a short time on convoy duty in the English Channel, and

Royal Navy

then proceeded to the Mediterranean. Calling at Gibraltar, thence to Malta, the *Lizard* was later in the engagement with the *Goeben* and the *Breslau* when these vessels made a dash from the Dardanelles in January 1918, the former being forced to run ashore, while the latter was sunk. He was also at the bombardment of Jaffa; was demobilised in February 1919.

THOMAS R. M'ARTHUR, Gunner, second son of Duncan M'Arthur, Merkland, who assisted his father on the farm and traded as a vegetable gardener, attested under the Derby Scheme in December 1915, and joined the Navy in March 1916. Called to Devonport in September 1916, he was in January 1917 sent on board the S.S. *Polzeath* in the Transport Service, a leading seaman and gunlayer. Submarines were frequently on their track, but, due to the vigilance and promptitude of the gunners, these pests were forced to submerge without effecting their purpose. Was demoblised in January 1919.

JAMES H. NICOL, A.B., a joiner in the Arran Estate workshop at Brodick Castle, only son of James Nicol, Cladoch, enlisted in October 1916, on attaining military age. He was trained at Devonport and drafted to H.M.S. *Royal Sovereign.* Obtaining his A.B. certificate, he was transferred in March 1918 to H.M.S. *Fox*, patrolling the Persian Gulf. Later, on service in the Caspian Sea after a long and arduous march to that quarter.

Brodick-Arran and the Great War

JAMES M'INTYRE, third son of William M'Intyre, Douglas Row, pluckily wanted to join the Army early in the war, when far below military age, but was prevented being accepted by his father approaching the local military representative. He afterwards, however, enlisted in the Navy when learning the blacksmith trade in Rothesay, and became a stoker on H.M.S. *Dido*.

CHARLES HENDRY, O.S., a joiner in the Arran Estate workshop at Brodick Castle, second son of David Hendry, Low Glencloy, enlisted in June 1916, but was not called up until January 1917, when he proceeded to Devonport, then to camp at Torr Point, Cornwall, and drafted in June 1917 as a seaman to H.M.S. *Suffolk* (cruiser), proceeding with her to the Far East. While there, after the Russian insurrection, he was one of a contingent of bluejackets landed at Vladivostock to co-operate with the Allied forces for the protection of life, property, and stores at that port. He is still in Eastern waters.

JAMES WILSON, A.B., eldest son of James Wilson, Douglas Row, was employed at Brodick Castle, and afterwards at timber-cutting in Perthshire, where he underwent a course of training as a Volunteer at Blair-Atholl. Joining the R.N.V. early in 1917, he was trained at the Crystal Palace, London, and has served on H.M.S. *Tiger*, *Repulse*, and *Hibernia*. Was in action in Heligoland Bight and off the Dogger Bank, and demobilised in February 1919.

Merchant Navy

JAMES B. M'ARTHUR, O.S., youngest son of Duncan M'Arthur, Merkland, was a gamekeeper in the employment of the Arran Estate at Dubhgharadh, and later went to timber-cutting in Perthshire. Trained as a Volunteer at Blair-Atholl from January 1916 to March 1917, he then joined the Royal Naval Volunteers and proceeded to the Crystal Palace, London. After a course of training there and at Chatham, he was sent as a seaman on board the *Lord Nelson* in the Mediterranean in September 1917.

JOHN DAVIDSON, youngest son of the late Robert Davidson, Glenrosa, an engineer to trade, working in one of the Clyde workshops, joined the Government oil-tank steamer *Rose Leaf* in autumn 1917, transferred later to the *Apple Leaf*. It may be interesting to note that his ship was engaged in escorting American troops to Britain, and also that he was present and saw the internment of the German Fleet at Scapa Flow. His ship was later serving with the destroyer squadron operating against the Bolsheviks in the Baltic.

Merchant Navy

JAMES HAMILTON, Captain, eldest son of the late Captain Adam Hamilton, Burnside, has been engaged in the Government Transport Service since the commencement of the war with the S.S. *Volumnia* owned by Gow, Harrison, & Co., Glasgow.

Brodick-Arran and the Great War

GEORGE and GAVIN HAMILTON, Captains, brothers of the above, have also been engaged in Government work with their steamers *River Cloy* and *Invercloy*, the former for a short time conveying mines to an American mine-layer in Lamlash, while the latter has been in attendance on the Fleet at Scapa Flow since early in the war.

ALEXANDER M'WATTIE, eldest son of James M'Wattie, 227 Paisley Road, Glasgow, and nephew of John M'Wattie, Low Glencloy, followed the sea as an occupation. On the outbreak of hostilities he joined the S.S. *Ardgower*, owned by Fulton & Lang, Greenock, which was taken over by the Admiralty. He was later transferred to the S.S. *Ardgarvel*, of which he was second officer, and in the winter of 1914 was engaged in the North Sea coaling vessels of the Fleet, trading afterwards to France.

For his vigilance in sighting a submarine he was awarded twenty pounds by the Admiralty. While on duty he unfortunately contracted a severe cold and died after a short illness in October 1918, aged 26 years.

WILLIAM FLECK, Engineer, eldest son of Captain William Fleck, pilot-master, Greenock, late of Brodick, joined the Transport Service in 1915, and served as third engineer on H.M. transports *Clutha* and *Hendon*, plying between Britain and France. Having been invalided to hospital, he died on 4th August 1918.

Royal Scots Greys

KENNETH CURRIE, third son of Archibald Currie, piermaster, joined the transport *Bhama*, of Patrick Henderson & Co., Glasgow, as an apprentice in June 1918.

WILLIAM CURRIE, second son of the aforesaid Archibald Currie, an engineer with Hastie & Co., Greenock, doing Admiralty work, joined the *Chindwin*, of Patrick Henderson & Co., as an engineer in the summer of 1918 engaged in Government work. While in the employ of Hastie & Co. he was sent out to superintend the fitting up of steering gear on submarines and patrol-boats.

Royal Scots Greys

JOHN S. CURRIE, Farrier-Quartermaster-Sergeant, second son of the late Archibald Currie, Douglas Row, was blacksmith at Lamlash, and attested on 18th November 1914. In consequence of having served in the Boer War, he was offered the rank of sergeant in the Black Watch, but from his experience as a trooper he preferred the cavalry, and a few weeks after attestation reported at the cavalry depot, Dunbar. After three months' training there, he was passed efficient and under orders to proceed to France in the next draft.

Meanwhile there was a great demand for efficient farriers with a thorough knowledge of horses and horse-shoeing, so he was transferred to the Army

Brodick-Arran and the Great War

Veterinary Corps on 22nd February 1915. Having passed all the necessary tests, he was offered the rank of farrier-staff-sergeant to remain in the home depot at Woolwich, but owing to his desire for service in the field he accepted instead the position of farrier-sergeant, and was put in charge of a hospital. Crossing to France on 28th May, he continued in this capacity until 21st February 1916, at which date he was promoted to the rank of farrier-staff-sergeant and transferred to a school of farriery as senior N.C.O. On 1st September following he was raised to the rank of farrier-quartermaster-sergeant, commonly known as farrier-major, a position that imposed on him the duty of lecturing to the men, instructing them in all details, examining all their work and being responsible for all the work done, as well as the discipline of the whole camp. Coming home on leave in February 1918, he reported sick, and after being in Stobhill Hospital, Glasgow, for about two months, underwent a serious operation, necessitating further treatment until 16th June 1918, when he received his discharge from the Army.

Scottish Horse

JAMES FINLAY, Lieutenant, 45th Battery R.F.A., joined the Scottish Horse (3rd) on 8th August 1914. Trained at Dunkeld, Morpeth, etc., he proceeded with his regiment to Gallipoli in August 1915. After a fortnight's sojourn there he was wounded

Scottish Horse

and sent to hospital in Malta. On recovery he was posted to Egypt, from which he proceeded to Salonica with the Camerons, to which he had been transferred. Again wounded, he was conveyed to Malta Hospital in December 1916, and returned home in March 1917 to take up a commission. After training at Exeter, he was gazetted to the R.F.A. in November 1917 and attached to the 45th Battery in the 3rd Division on the Western front, where he took part in many severe actions until the Armistice, having been in twenty battles since 1st August 1918.

He acted as Captain of the Battery from 15th September 1918.

Previous to enlisting, Lieutenant Finlay was a member of the Arran Estate Office staff. He is a native of Winchburgh, Linlithgow, and was demobilised in January 1919.

WILLIAM STEWART, Douglas Row, a painter in the joiner's department at Brodick Castle, elder son of the late John Stewart, Invercloy, attested under the Derby Scheme and passed for home service, was called up in January 1917, and sent on to Sutton-on-Sea, Lincolnshire, for training, finishing off at Alford in the Signal Section. On 12th July 1917 he was posted to the Agricultural Company at Lincoln, and sent to Grantham, where he was seventeen months on a farm, being afterwards transferred to Brodick Castle Farm. Was demobilised in February 1919.

Brodick-Arran and the Great War

Lovat Scouts

DOUGLAS JOSS, Lance-Corporal, son-in-law of William Walker, Invercloy, employed in the Duke of Sutherland's Estate Office, Golspie, enlisted in August 1914. Trained on the Lincoln and Norfolk coasts, he was sent to Gallipoli in August 1915, and engaged at Suvla Bay from September to December inclusive. Invalided with enteric fever, he was in hospital in Malta and Aberdeen from January to April 1916, when he rejoined his regiment. Transferred to the Camerons in November 1916, he was sent to France, and engaged on the Somme front until March 1917, at which date he was invalided with trench fever, and treated in the 14th Stationary Hospital, Boulogne, Stoke-on-Trent War Hospital, and Churchfields Convalescent Hospital, West Bromwich. Reporting at the depot, Invergordon, he was drafted to France again in September 1917, and engaged on the Nieuport-Dunkirk front, afterwards on the Cambrian front. Wounded in leg and contracting trench feet, he was, about the beginning of January 1918, conveyed to Beaufort Hospital, Bristol. In March 1918 he rejoined his regiment in Ireland, and in April following was transferred to the Machine Gun Corps, 6th Battalion, at Grantham, and later at the School of Instruction. Demobilised in February 1919.

JOHN ANDERSON, a native of Perthshire, an under-

Lovat Scouts

gamekeeper at Brodick Castle, enlisted on 5th November 1914. Trained at Kimbolton and Thetford, he proceeded in a draft to Gallipoli on 7th September 1915. After a spell on the peninsula, he was invalided to Egypt, and on recovery joined his regiment there. Owing to a recurrence of illness while at Salonica, he came home to Britain in 1917, and after short leave, rejoined the Cameron Highlanders, to which the Scouts had been transferred, and crossed to France in the summer of 1918, where he was serving at the time of the Armistice. He was later in Germany, and demobilised in February 1919.

JOHN MITCHELL, a gardener at Brodick Castle, and a native of Calgary, Island of Mull, enlisted on 5th November 1914. After training at Kimbolton and Thetford, he sailed for Gallipoli on 7th September 1915. He went through the fighting on the peninsula, and after serving in Egypt, was transferred to Salonica, where he was wounded and sent to this country. Drafted, on recovery, into the 6th Camerons, he was engaged on the Western front, and again wounded in 1917, and sent to hospital in Paisley. Returning to the depot at Nigg, he was sent to France again in June 1918, and killed in action on 8th August.

DUGALD M'KILLOP, an under-gamekeeper at Brodick Castle, enlisted on 5th November 1914, and after training at Kimbolton and Thetford, was

Brodick-Arran and the Great War

drafted on 7th September 1915 to the Eastern war zone on board the S.S. *Andania*. Calling at Malta and Alexandria, they eventually arrived at Mudros, where they were transferred into smaller boats and taken to Gallipoli, landing there on the night of 26th September 1915. He continued on the peninsula until the evacuation at Suvla on 19th December 1915, being then conveyed to Embros, where, after a few days' stay, they embarked for Alexandria, arriving there on 27th December. Here they rested for a week, and were afterwards encamped beside the Pyramids for about a month. After serving six months on outpost duty in the desert, the Scouts returned to Cairo, where they were converted into a battalion of Cameron Highlanders (10th Lovat Scouts Battalion), and a few weeks later embarked at Alexandria for Salonica on 17th October 1916, landing there on the 20th, and after a week's march up country they entered the firing line. Taking over a sector in Macedonia opposite Seres, and serving later in other sectors on this front, they were relieved by the Greeks on 20th June 1918, and left Salonica for France, where they arrived in the first week of July and were formed into an observation battalion. He was demobilised in February 1919. During his service abroad he had never been wounded nor in hospital from sickness, although he had a slight touch of the dreaded malaria. He is a native of Perthshire.

D. K. LINDSAY, Corporal, a gamekeeper by pro-

Lovat Scouts

fession, son of Robert Lindsay, gamekeeper, Dippen, and son-in-law of Duncan M'Arthur, Merkland, enlisted on 5th November 1914. Also trained at Kimbolton and Thetford, he sailed with M'Killop, Anderson, and Mitchell for Gallipoli on 7th September 1915, and engaged there until the evacuation; afterwards in Egypt, and in Salonica until June 1918, when he was transferred to France in company with M'Killop, with whom he had been associated throughout the campaign and demobilised at the same time.

JOHN K. LANGLANDS, Farrier-Sergeant, elder son of Dugald Langlands, Invercloy, was a blacksmith in the employ of Miss Currie, Rosaburn. Enlisting on 5th November 1914, he was posted to the first reserve regiment at Kimbolton, thence to Thetford, later to Hoxne, Lowestoft, and Langley Park, Norwich. The Scouts then became a cycle regiment and went to Somerleyton Park, near Lowestoft, where he witnessed a bombardment by the enemy on 26th April 1916. Stationed later at Gorleston, Yarmouth, he there saw the grand and unique spectacle of a Zeppelin being brought down.

The Scouts having now been converted into an infantry regiment supplying drafts to the 1/7 Camerons in France, he was transferred to the R.F.A. on 27th January 1917, and sent to the 1203 Lowland Battery stationed in Deal. Having been to several other camps, he was subsequently sent to Woolwich for overseas, but as farriers were

Brodick-Arran and the Great War

not in demand, was drafted to a remount depot, Welling, Kent, and later to the 2/1 Renfrewshire Battery at Aylsham, Norfolk, for coast defence. Moved to other camps, he was again sent to Woolwich on 24th October 1918 for overseas, and while there was put on the Staff. Demobilised in February 1919.

JOHN CURRIE, a local postman, nephew of Archibald Currie, Rowan Bank, enlisted on 22nd November 1915 as a shoeing smith, and left Brodick for Oakley Park on 1st December, thence to Lowestoft in February following, from which he went later to Somerleyton and Herringfleet-hall. Having been transferred to the R.F.A., he was in Maryhill Barracks, Glasgow, from June to 31st October 1917, when he was removed to Bettesfield Camp, Wales. From here he was drafted to France on 4th May 1918, and posted to the 16th Battery, 41st Brigade, with which he was until invalided down the line about 8th November from near Mons and taken to hospital in Birmingham. Demobilised in February 1919.

ALEXANDER FRASER, Sergeant, No. 1 Group, Lovat Scouts Sharpshooters, a native of Daviot, Inverness-shire, was head gamekeeper at Brodick Castle, and attested under the Derby Scheme in December 1915. Called up in July 1916, most of his training was undertaken at St Andrews, on completion of which he was sent to the Western

Lovat Scouts

front as sergeant in charge of the first group of sharpshooters on 9th October 1916. This group, under Sergeant Fraser's charge, have had many vicissitudes, but they have proved their worth when mention is made that the following distinctions have been won by them—viz., one D.C.M., one M.S.M., and five M.M.'s, Sergeant Fraser being decorated with the M.S.M. for his continuous good work. The sergeant served with the Lovat Scouts during the Boer War for one and a half years, and holds the Queen's Medal and three clasps, as well as the honour of being made a Burgess of Inverness. He was gassed slightly on two occasions in France. Demobilised in March 1919.

ALEXANDER S. M'FARLANE, No. 1 Group, Lovat Scouts Sharpshooters, was deer-stalker at Brodick Castle, and attested under the Derby Scheme in December 1915. He joined the Army on 17th July 1916, and trained at Scone, St Andrews, and Beauly; proceeded with the group to France, landing at Boulogne on 10th October 1916. Six days later he was on duty in the firing line at Loos, and was subsequently engaged in battle at Arras, Vimy Ridge, Hill 65, and Hill 70. Like the other members of the group, he had many exciting experiences, and for his good work at Hill 70 on 15th August 1917, was awarded the Military Medal. On 20th May 1917 he was wounded slightly at Vimy Ridge.

Taking ill, he was invalided on 4th January 1918 from the 24th General Hospital, France, to Ford House

Brodick-Arran and the Great War

Military Hospital, Devonport, transferred on 20th April to Bellahouston Red Cross Hospital, Glasgow, thence to Lamlash Auxiliary Hospital on 20th May, and back to Bellahouston on 20th November, from which he was discharged for duty on 20th December, and reported at Lovat Scout Headquarters at Beauly on 30th December 1918. During active service he was attached to the First Army on the Lens-La Bassée front. He is a native of the Trossachs, Perthshire. Demobilised in January 1919.

6th Dragoon Guards

SIMON LAWSON, Trooper, reservist, employed as a carriage-driver with Miss Currie, Rosaburn, having been mobilised on the declaration of war, took part in the early stages of the fighting in Flanders, where he was wounded on 30th October 1914. Captured later by the Germans, he became a prisoner of war until August 1915, when he was released and sent home with a batch of prisoners from Germany. On his return he became an inmate of Wandsworth Hospital, and was discharged after a fortnight's treatment for bullet wounds in his arm and leg. Unfortunately, he had not been long at his home in Glasgow when he was accidentally shot in the street, and subsequently died, due to the carelessness of a soldier on furlough riding on a tram-car with a loaded rifle, which went off as he picked it up preparatory to leaving the car.

Royal Highlanders (Black Watch)

Royal Highlanders (Black Watch)

GEORGE GOLDTHORPE, Sergeant, porter and postman at Brodick Castle, a native of Barton-on-Humber, enlisted in the 9th Battalion on 7th September 1914. After training at Aldershot and other centres in England, he went to France in the spring of 1915, and took part in several minor actions previous to the battle of Loos on 25th September 1915, where he was killed. Before coming to Brodick Castle, Goldthorpe served in the Navy, and while on the China Station took part in the Boxer Revolution, for which he held medal and clasp.

MALCOLM M'ARTHUR, employed in the forestry department at Brodick Castle, eldest son of Duncan M'Arthur, Merkland, enlisted on 7th September 1914 in the 9th Battalion. When training at Aldershot, he was discharged in April 1915 with a bad ankle. Subsequently he worked in a coal mine at Shotts, and in January 1918 joined the Motor Transport Service, and trained in London and Bedford. Later he was transferred to the Army Reserve, and is now with the Board of Trade Timber Supply Company at Dalrymple, Ayrshire.

JOHN M'ALLISTER, adopted son of James M'Allister, Fir Cottage, joined the Colours on 7th September 1915. Trained in the 9th Battalion at

Brodick-Arran and the Great War

Aldershot and surrounding districts, the battalion crossed to France in the spring of 1915. He was in the firing line from July till the battle of Loos, at which he was killed on 25th September 1915. Prior to enlisting, he was employed in the forestry department at Brodick Castle.

WILLIAM M'INTYRE, a gardener at Brodick Castle, second son of William M'Intyre, Douglas Row, enlisted at the same time as M'Allister and Goldthorpe; they trained together, went to France together, and were all killed at the battle of Loos. M'Intyre was only 19 years of age.

DAVID M'AUSLAN, Sergeant-Major, elder son of David M'Auslan, Douglas Row, late head gardener at Brodick Castle, was a gardener in the employ of the Earl of Southesk, Kinnaird Castle, Forfarshire, and enlisted on 12th August 1914. Promoted to sergeant in 1915, he was appointed sergeant-instructor in 191st Infantry Brigade School of Instruction for N.C.O.'s in March 1916; transferred in the same capacity in 1917 to Northern Army School of Instruction, Newmarket; early in 1918 to Combined Schools at Brandon; and in July 1918 appointed sergeant-major in N.C.O.'s School of Instruction at Thetford.

ALEXANDER WILSON, a carter employed with William Currie, Douglas Row, enlisted in the 9th Battalion in September 1914; was engaged in the

Royal Highlanders (Black Watch)

battle of Loos and subsequent fighting, and later in the Transport Department.

DAVID LINDSAY, Sergeant, a gardener at Brodick Castle, joined the 10th Battalion on 8th October 1914. He trained at Sutton Veny and Bristol, and went with the battalion to France about the middle of September 1915. After a few months, the battalion was transferred to the Eastern front, and he served with the Salonica Forces continuously since. Although he took part in engagements in both spheres of activity, he was fortunate enough to have escaped without injury. He is a native of Crieff, Perthshire.

JOHN GILLIES, a joiner at Brodick Castle, younger son of Malcolm Gillies, Glenriggart, enlisted on 8th October 1914. Trained in the 10th Battalion at Sutton Veny and Bristol, he was sent to France about the middle of September 1915. After two months there he was invalided, and while in hospital his battalion had been transferred to the Eastern front; so on recovery he was posted to the 8th Battalion, in the 9th Division, with which he served continuously down to the cessation of hostilities, taking part in much hard fighting at the Somme, Arras, Ypres, and various other parts, without injury, although he had many narrow escapes. He was recently home on leave, having left his regiment at the historic town of Liège on its way to the Rhine, rejoining later in Germany.

Brodick-Arran and the Great War

PETER CURRIE, an employee in the forestry department at Brodick Castle, youngest son of the late Archibald Currie, Douglas Row, enlisted as a piper in the 11th Battalion on 20th November 1914. Trained at Nigg and Tain, he was, after relinquishing his duties as piper by his own desire, drafted to France as a private on 18th August 1915, and attached to the 9th Battalion at Hazebrouck. His first experience in the firing-line was at Hooge a few days later. Relieved by a Canadian Division on the evening of the 29th, the 15th Division, of which the 9th Battalion was a unit, was moved to the Loos-Lens sector, and eventually took part in the memorable battle of Loos on 25th September, when, after being four and a half hours in the deadly combat, he was wounded through the right forearm by a bullet. From a field hospital at Lillers he was sent to Le Havre, thence to Southampton, and on to the 3rd General Hospital, Birmingham; subsequently transferred to Coventry Military Hospital, and later to a Convalescent Military Hospital at Eastbourne. Discharged from there on 24th November, he went, after a few days' home leave, into camp at Catterick, and sailed for the East from Devonport on 14th February 1916, arriving at Basrah on 11th March. He afterwards took part in the abortive attempt to relieve Kut, when he was severely wounded on the right shoulder and hands by a shell from the British guns falling short, as well as by machine-gun fire of the enemy, while he with others was on night patrol duty close

Royal Highlanders (Black Watch)

to the Turkish trenches. Here he lay for four hours before being picked up and taken to the Indian Field Hospital, where he had one of his fingers amputated by an Indian doctor, being afterwards conveyed to hospital in Basrah, thence to Colaba Field Hospital, Bombay. Leaving there on 24th May, he was admitted into hospital at Alexandria, which he left for England on 12th June, landing at Southampton on the 24th. Taken to Southwark Military Hospital, London, he was in due course transferred to Stanwell House Convalescent Home, Sutton, Surrey, and discharged from the Army on 19th September 1916, being unfit for further military service. He subsequently took up duty again in the forestry department at Brodick Castle.

ARCHIBALD M'BRIDE, a local coal agent, elder son of the late John M'Bride, High Glencloy, enlisted in the 11th Battalion on 18th November 1914. Trained at Nigg, Tain, Richmond, and Grantham, he was transferred at the latter place to the Machine Gun Corps in the end of November 1915, and went from Grantham to Preston in December following. Back to Grantham again in February 1916, he was sent to France on 6th March, and served with the 25th Battalion.

The Machine Gun Battalion, since the 18th February 1918, has been engaged among other places at the Somme, Ploegsteert, Kemmel, Aisne, Marcatel, etc., and from 21st February to 11th

Brodick-Arran and the Great War

November 1918 the battalion has gained the following honours:—D.S.O., 2; M.C., 9; D.C.M., 11; M.M., 68; M.S.M., 1; mentioned in despatches, 7; French decorations, 3. He was demobilised in March 1919.

NORMAN SILLARS, Sergeant, 9th Battalion, an electrical engineer in Glasgow, fourth son of Robert Sillars, East Knowe, joined the Army in July 1916. Trained at Nigg, he was drafted to France in December following, and wounded in the leg on 9th April 1917. After recovering, he crossed to France again in August, and was wounded in the hand in the great German offensive in March 1918; was in an English hospital until June, and after a short spell at a convalescent camp in Ireland, he was sent to France again in July, and later in the First Army Infantry School there.

JOHN SKELTON, eldest son of the late John Skelton, Low Glencloy, enlisted in August 1917, and is in the 2nd Battalion. He was previously employed on the Arran roads and at timber-cutting in Perthshire, when he trained as a Volunteer at Blair-Atholl. Trained at Nigg, he was sent out to India, and in the spring of 1918 transferred to Egypt. Later he was on service in Mesopotamia, and invalided to hospital in Cairo in the autumn shortly before the Armistice.

Cameron Highlanders

DAVID ADAM, Lieutenant, employed as a timekeeper with Messrs David Rowan & Co., engineers and boilermakers, Glasgow, third son of David Adam, formerly grieve on West Mayish Farm, was a sergeant in the 5th Battalion Scottish Rifles (Territorials) and enlisted as a private in the 7th Camerons on 7th September 1914. He was promoted to lance-corporal on 18th September; sergeant on 28th September; company sergeant-major on 12th November; 2nd lieutenant on 26th March 1917; lieutenant on 1st September 1918, and attached to a Labour corps at Salonica. Severely wounded at Loos on 25th September 1915 by bullet through right arm, he was taken to Northumberland War Hospital, Gosforth, Newcastle-on-Tyne.

Wounded again in France on 27th September 1917 by shrapnel and lost left eye, he was treated in Whitworth Street Hospital, Manchester. He had the honour of being mentioned in Sir John French's despatch, Loos, September 1915. Of a martial spirit, he had previously been in active service in the Balkan War with the Scottish Ambulance Unit.

ANDREW EDWARD WATSON, Sergeant, son of Alexander Watson, 74 Dundrennan Road, Glasgow, late of Brodick, was employed in the counting-house of Messrs George M'Lellan & Sons, Glasgow Rubber Works, Maryhill, Glasgow. He enlisted in

Brodick-Arran and the Great War

the 4th Battalion (Territorials) on 20th March 1913, and mobilised at the outbreak of war. After training in Bedford, the battalion was sent to France on 19th February, and he served on various parts of the line, including Armentières, La Bassée, Loos, Vermelles, and Albert. His first engagement was Neuve Chapelle on 10th March 1915, when he was wounded by shrapnel on the scalp and taken to hospital at Rouen. Afterwards engaged at Aubers Ridge on 9th May, Festubert on the 17th and 18th, when the battalion greatly distinguished itself; he was later at Loos from 25th September to 1st October.

Subsequently the battalion was disbanded, and in February 1918 he found himself in the 7th Battalion, and in November following, when hostilities ceased, was employed at office work in Rouen.

PETER DAVIDSON, fourth son of the late Robert Davidson, Glenrosa, employed with Messrs A. Wooley & Son, Brodick, enlisted early in September 1917 in the 5th Battalion (Lochiel's). Trained principally at Aldershot, he was sent to France in May 1915 and severely wounded in left arm, shoulder, and chest at Loos, 25th September 1915. The battalion went into action about 850 strong, and out of that number the colonel and only a small proportion of officers and men survived. After about six months' treatment in a Nottingham hospital, he was discharged from the Army in March 1916, and subsequently assisted in the work of the farm.

Cameron Highlanders

SAMUEL M'ECHRAN, in the employ of Miss Currie, merchant, Invercloy, enlisted in September 1914. Trained in Inverness and various centres in England, he crossed to France in July 1915. He has had a varied experience, having been engaged in the Transport Department looking after the colonel's horses as well as a share of active warfare. He served in the 6th Battalion. Demobilised in March 1919.

ALEXANDER DAVIDSON, Corporal, third son of the late Robert Davidson, Glenrosa, was an ironmonger in Dingwall, where he attested under the Derby Scheme. Called up in April 1916, he joined the 4th Camerons, and was a bombing instructor while training in Norfolk. Sent to France in the early summer of 1917, and transferred to the 6th Battalion, he was wounded by bullet through the right hand in the attack on the German trenches during the third battle of Ypres, 31st July 1917.

After recovery he was for a spell in Ireland, and in the spring of 1918 was transferred to London to learn motor-driving. Afterwards in France in that capacity, he was seriously injured by a motor collision on 25th August 1918, having had his leg badly fractured and several ribs broken as well. He was conveyed to the General Military Hospital, Edmonton, London, of which he is still an inmate.

ANGUS DEWAR, who had enlisted at an early stage of hostilities, was killed at Arras in April 1917. He was the third son of the late John Dewar, at one time head gamekeeper at Brodick Castle, and had been for a considerable time on service.

Argyll and Sutherland Highlanders

DAVID F. GILLIES, Corporal, youngest son of Daniel Gillies, 30 Montgomerie Street, Ardrossan, and grandson of the late William Mowatt, Millhouse, Brodick, was a ship's draughtsman with the Fairfield Shipbuilding Co., Ltd., and enlisted in the 4th Battalion on 28th August 1914. Trained at Plymouth, he was drafted to France on 13th July 1915, and there joined the 2nd Battalion. Holding the line at La Bassée, he was engaged with the battalion at Loos on 25th September, the casualties in killed, wounded, and missing being 641 out of 800 men. Things were comparatively quiet until 25th January 1916, when the battalion, supported by the 5th Scottish Rifles, repulsed a very heavy attack, with great losses to the enemy. Returning from leave and rejoining the battalion in May following, it was moved to the Somme, and relieved the French at Fricourt about the middle of June. Here an intense bombardment was put up by the British for several days, and in the opening days of July they advanced five miles, but got hung up at Metize Wood, which they eventually took, with a large number of prisoners. After very heavy fighting at Highwood on the 18th, resulting in heavy casualties, they attacked at another part on the 26th, but after

Argyll and Sutherland Highlanders

taking the enemy trenches, were cut off. Volunteers having been called for to try and get through for assistance, he and six privates set out, but they were picked off one by one, and he was left alone in the perilous undertaking. After six eventful hours, however, he managed through to the supporting battalion, the Glasgow Highlanders, which immediately advanced and succeeded in rescuing their comrades in the third attack. At this juncture Corporal Gillies was wounded by a bullet through the right side of his face, another passing through a small Testament in his breast-pocket. Having been a month in hospital at Rouen, he rejoined the battalion early in October 1916, when he had the satisfaction of being told by the Commanding Officer that he had won the Military Medal for his bravery. Continuing with the battalion until June 1917, he was then presented with the medal in London by Sir Archibald Hunter, and from that date was sent to work at his usual occupation, being still in the Army Reserve until 14th December 1917, when he was discharged.

GEORGE RESIDE, Corporal, employed by Messrs Wilkie & Kennedy, wholesale drapers, 34 Osborne Street, Glasgow, elder son of John Reside, 181 New City Road, Glasgow, late of Brodick, enlisted in the 4th Battalion in May 1916. Trained at Redford Barracks, Edinburgh, he crossed to France in March 1917, was transferred to the 1/7 Gordons, and killed on 23rd April, near Arras. He was in his nineteenth year.

Brodick-Arran and the Great War

THOMAS ADAM, pastry baker with James Craig, baker and confectioner, Glasgow, fourth son of David Adam, Glasgow, late of Brodick, enlisted on 8th May 1916 in the 13th Battalion. Wounded in France on 24th April 1917 by bullet and shrapnel in ankle and shin bones, he was taken to Northumberland War Hospital, Gosforth, Newcastle-on-Tyne. He was wounded in France again by shrapnel in the leg on 28th March 1918, and treated in General Hospital, France. Wounded for the third time in France on 26th August 1918 by shrapnel in the knee and neck, he was again an inmate of the General Hospital, France.

ANDREW WATSON, Skelton, second son of the late John Skelton, Low Glencloy, was variously employed, and enlisted in June 1916. After training in Edinburgh, he was sent to France in September 1916; was wounded in October 1917, and subsequently in Ireland. In May 1918 he was transferred to the Northumberland Fusiliers, afterwards joining the Machine Gun Corps, and again sent to France towards the end of September 1918. Demobilised in January 1919.

MALCOLM ALEXANDER MITCHELL, son-in-law of the late Thomas Reid, schoolmaster, employed as a ship steward, enlisted in September 1916. Sent to Norwich, he was at the beginning of October put to farm work at Gorleston-on-Sea for six weeks. Trained at Norwich and Taverham Camp in the

Argyll and Sutherland Highlanders

2/6 Battalion, he was drafted to France in August 1917, and there transferred to the 11th Battalion. On 17th November 1917 he was posted missing after a raiding exploit, and in August 1918 was officially presumed dead on the date he went amissing, or since.

ROBERT SILLARS, second son of Robert Sillars, East Knowe, was variously employed, and enlisted in October 1916. Trained at Colinton, near Edinburgh, he embarked for Salonica in January 1917. He had been in hospital there with an attack of dysentery, and in November 1918 returned from the front to hospital in Salonica with an injured foot. He was serving in the 12th Battalion.

CHARLES HENDERSON, Invercloy, third son of Donald Henderson, Birchvale, a gardener by profession, employed by the Brodick Public Hall Company as hallkeeper and bowling-green keeper, attested under the Derby Scheme and was called up in January 1917. While training in Kent he was sent to farm work at Lockerbie, afterwards in Kirkcudbrightshire. Demobilised in February 1919.

ANGUS M'NICOL, second son of Colin M'Nicol, Douglas Row, was an apprentice baker with Messrs A. Wooley & Son, and had been exempted for a few months after attaining to military age. Called up in the middle of May 1918, he was trained in Edinburgh and Dunbar, and sent to France on 4th

Brodick-Arran and the Great War

October. Invalided early in 1919 to hospital in Newcastle-on-Tyne, he died there on 9th March, and was interred in Brodick Churchyard, the first of the local soldiers buried at home.

Royal Scots Fusiliers

DUNCAN M'INTYRE, Corporal, brother of Mrs Kelly, Douglas Row, although not generally resident in the locality, comes and goes a good deal. Previous to the war he had been employed in the forestry department at Brodick Castle, but at the outbreak of war was a gardener with Mr Kirkpatrick, Whiting Bay. He joined the Colours early, having enlisted on 15th August 1914. Trained at Aldershot and surrounding district in the 6th Battalion with the 9th Scottish Division, he went to France with that division in May 1915. Engaged at the battle of Loos, 25th September 1915, and in the fierce fighting for the Hohenzollern Redoubt in the days following, he was at the Somme from August 1916 till February 1917 and took part in the capture of Martinpuich, the first action in which tanks were used. He was also engaged at Arras on 9th April 1917; Cavalry Farm, 23rd April 1917; Ypres, August 1917; and in hard fighting at Zonnebeke in this month. Holding the line at Bullecourt when the Germans launched their offensive on 21st March 1918, he was at the capture of the village of Meteren in July following, and took part in the fighting at Ypres on 28th

Royal Scots Fusiliers

September 1918, the beginning of the offensive in Belgium, when the Germans were gradually pushed back and the coast of Belgium once more free. He was once buried and once wounded, having had his foot bruised, for which he was treated in No. 3 Canadian General Hospital, Boulogne. He served with the 9th and 15th Scottish Divisions, also the 59th Division, and was with the 2nd Battalion, 9th Division, in Germany. Demobilised in March 1919.

NEIL GILLIES, elder son of Malcolm Gillies, Glenriggart, was employed with Messrs J. & P. Coats, Ltd., Paisley, and enlisted on 10th September 1914. Trained in the 8th Battalion at Sutton Veny and Bristol, he went to France about 20th September 1915, and proceeded to Bray, thence to Ploegsteert, and later was at Loos, Arras, Vimy Ridge, Kemmel, Meteren, Amiens, St Quentin, Ypres, Cambrai, etc. He was thrice wounded—first at the Somme in July 1916, then on the Cambrai front in March 1917, and lastly at Ypres on 30th September 1918, and treated respectively in Sudbury Hospital, Suffolk, Bellevue War Hospital, Bristol, and 3rd Canadian General Hospital, Boulogne. After leaving Boulogne he was sent on to Germany, where he rejoined his battalion, the 9th Scottish Rifles, to which he had been transferred in 1917. Demobilised in January 1919.

HUGH MILLER REID, second son of the late Thomas Reid, schoolmaster, Brodick, was a gardener with Miss Beckett, Glenfoot, Ardrossan, and enlisted in June 1916. Trained at Fort Matilda, he was sent to France in October following, and after one year and six months on active service, died of pneumonia in the spring of 1917 in hospital at Etaples, and was buried there.

Scottish Rifles

FREDERICK J. DEACON, Lieutenant, only son of W. W. H. Deacon and the late Jessie R. Deacon, Manchester, and nephew of the Misses Robertson, 29 Keir Street, Pollokshields, Glasgow, and Millburn, Lamlash, was a shipbroker in Glasgow, and enlisted early in September 1914 in the 9th Battalion H.L.I. (Glasgow Highlanders). He has a close connection with Brodick on the maternal side, and is a near relative of the writer. Trained at Dunfermline and Stirling, he was dispatched to France on 26th June 1915, and served with the 9th Battalion in the La Bassée sector and the Somme until December 1916.

During that time he went through the fighting on the Somme from July 1916 to December, having been engaged in the attacks at Highwood on 15th July, Delville Wood on 23rd August, also at Le Transloy on 4th November.

Coming home in December 1916 to study for a commission, he was sent to the 18th O.C.B. at Bath; was gazetted to the 7th Scottish Rifles on 28th May 1917; returned to France as 2nd lieutenant in that

Scottish Rifles

battalion on 13th April 1918, attached to the 52nd Division.

Wounded at Marcatel, near Arras, in the British offensive of 24th August following, he was, after initial treatment in France, conveyed to the Prince of Wales Hospital, London, and towards the end of September sent convalescent to Moffat, where he was kept, however, only a few days, having been granted home leave; but unfortunately he contracted a chill, and when hostilities ceased, found himself an inmate of Yorkhill Hospital, Glasgow. He is now in charge of the Scottish Rifle Detachment at the depot, Forthside, Stirling.

THOMAS LAING, Corporal, chemist, Glasgow, son-in-law of Donald Henderson, Birchvale, Brodick, enlisted in the 7th Battalion in October 1914. Trained at Grangemouth, he was sent to Gallipoli on 13th May 1915, and wounded on 12th July following. Taken to hospital in Alexandria, and thence to Manchester, Moisley Hall, and Stobhill, he was subsequently sent to Randalston as camp dispenser in August 1916, and in February 1918 moved to Nigg, where he now is.

ALEXANDER BRUCE, Sergeant, second son of John Bruce, Sannox, and nephew of Mrs Dugald Langlands, Invercloy, enlisted in the 3/5 Battalion in May 1915. He underwent training at Glasgow and at Hipswell Camp, Catterick, Yorkshire. Unfortunately, he was killed in France on 23rd April

Brodick-Arran and the Great War

1917, having only been about six weeks at the front.

Previous to enlisting, he was a steward on board Sir Thomas Glen Coats' yacht *Hebe*. He was sergeant of the officers' mess before going to France.

T. F. WOOLEY, Lance-Corporal, only son of Thomas Wooley, Tain, and nephew of Alexander Wooley, Invercloy, enlisted in the Motor Transport Service in January 1917, but in March following was transferred to the 3rd Scottish Rifles.

Trained at Invergordon, he was drafted to France in March 1918 and took part in the fighting at Cambrai and Mount Kemmel.

Invalided in June with trench fever, he was taken to the 1st General Northern Hospital, Newcastle, subsequently to a convalescent hospital in Durham. Afterwards at Scottish Command depot at Nigg, and passed fit early in December.

Royal Scots

JOHN JOYCE, Sergeant, an under-gamekeeper at Brodick Castle, enlisted on 7th September 1914. After training at various centres in Scotland and England, he went with his regiment to the Western front in the spring of 1915. He was transferred later to the Eastern, and being wounded in an engagement in Egypt on 19th July 1916, he subsequently died in Cairo. He was a native of Lauder.

Royal Scots

ALEXANDER M'KAY, Lieutenant, sub-factor on the Earl of Wemyss' Scottish estates, and son-in-law of Alexander Wooley, Invercloy, was gazetted a 2nd lieutenant, and joined the 3/8 Battalion on 9th December 1915. Trained at Peebles, Craiglockhart, Stobs, and Catterick, he went to France on 5th January 1917 and there joined the 8th Battalion, in the 51st Division, at Ovillers, in the Somme district. After a few days the battalion went back for a short rest to Le Plessiel, a small village near Abbeville, subsequently moving up to the Arras sector, and billeted in the ruined town of Arras, doing routine and trench work in this area for some time. On 9th April they took part in that very successful Arras push of the Third Army which forced the Germans back some six miles in a day and a half, the particular place in which they were engaged being just to the right of Vimy Ridge. After a brief rest they again went into the line in the same sector in the vicinity of the famous chemical works near Roeux, which changed hands some four times in a week. Towards the end of May the division was again withdrawn for a short spell to Bonninquex, a village near St Omer, moving afterwards to Flanders, the Ypres sector, and billeted in dug-outs on the Yser canal bank. Holding now the rank of 1st lieutenant, he took part with the division in the advance of about 5 miles, which commenced on 31st July, towards Poelcappelle. From this neighbourhood he was invalided down the line and conveyed to England on 23rd November 1917. After about two months in No. 25 General Hospital, Hardelot, he was placed on home service duty and attached to Infantry Command Depot, Catterick, where he is adjutant of the Scottish wing of the depot.

Highland Light Infantry

HUGH M'WATTIE, Sergeant, second son of James M'Wattie, 227 Paisley Road, Glasgow, and nephew of John M'Wattie, Low Glencloy, was a postman in Glasgow. Having joined the Territorials, the 9th Battalion (Glasgow Highlanders), in March 1914, he was mobilised on 4th August and sent to Dunfermline for training. While there he volunteered for foreign service, and crossed to France on 15th January 1915, subsequently taking part in much fighting. Promoted to lance-corporal in May, he was engaged in the battle of the Somme in July 1916, was wounded at Highwood, and taken to hospital in Leeds. Returning to France in February 1917, he was made a corporal in May following, and promoted to sergeant shortly afterwards. Wounded again during the British retreat in March 1918, he was taken to hospital in Boulogne, rejoined his battalion in May, and while holding the lines was gassed and slightly wounded in June, and conveyed to hospital in Norwich. Afterwards in Catterick Camp. Besides heavy fighting at La Bassée, Loos, Polygon Wood, Armentières, the breaking of the Hindenburg Line,

Highland Light Infantry

etc., he took part in many other engagements and raids.

JOHN M'WATTIE, Lance-Corporal, younger brother of the above, and an apprentice blacksmith with Messrs A. & W. Smith, Engineers, Glasgow, joined the same regiment on the same date as his brother. Mobilised on 4th August 1914, he was sent to Dunfermline, afterwards to Edinburgh, and later to Deal, in Kent. Having been confined to hospital in Edinburgh for some time, he was retained for home service; but while in Kent he volunteered for foreign service, and was sent to France in June 1917. Holding the rank now of lance-corporal, he was wounded at Passchendaele in both legs and both arms. Both legs having been amputated, he lived for sixteen days, and died on 16th December 1917 at No. 1 Clearing Station, France.

NEIL T. CURRIE, 2nd Lieutenant, eldest son of Archibald Currie, piermaster, a clerk in the marine insurance office of Messrs Robert Law, Cuthbert & Co., Glasgow, enlisted in the Glasgow Chamber of Commerce Battalion (the 17th) at its inception in September 1914. Trained at Troon, Prees Heath, Wensley Dale, Totley, and Codford, he embarked with the battalion at Southampton for France in November 1915. Taking part in the battle of the Somme on 1st July 1916 and successive engagements without injury, he was afterwards on duty at the base for a considerable time, and in

Brodick-Arran and the Great War

November 1917 obtained a commission in a Labour battalion in France.

ALEXANDER FLECK, Lance-Sergeant, formerly an officer in the Transport Service, youngest son of Captain William Fleck, pilot-master, Greenock, late of Brodick, joined the 16th Battalion on 23rd September 1914. Trained at Gailes and Codford, he crossed to France in November 1915, and was unfortunately killed at Albert on 1st July 1916. He gained the Military Medal.

JOHN BARBOUR, eldest son of James Barbour, Douglas Row, who was employed on Brodick Pier, enlisted in the Glasgow Chamber of Commerce Battalion on 15th September 1914. After training at Troon, etc., he crossed to France with the battalion in November 1915, and was on active service until invalided to England and operated on for appendicitis on 27th April 1916, in Manchester Royal Infirmary. Returning to France on 20th August 1916, after being in Montrose since June, he was attached to the Transport Department of the 16th Battalion. Was demobilised early in March 1919, after being on duty beyond the Rhine.

JAMES BARBOUR, younger brother of the above, employed in the forestry department at Brodick Castle, enlisted in the same battalion in November 1914. Also trained at Troon, etc., he accompanied the battalion to France in November 1915, and

Highland Light Infantry

was killed at Thiepval in the fighting at the Somme on 1st July 1916. He was only 21 years of age.

JOHN FLECK, clerk, employed with Messrs Bulloch, Lade & Co., Glasgow, second son of Captain William Fleck, pilot - master, Greenock, joined the 6th Battalion in November 1914. Trained at Durdygates, he was sent to Gallipoli in May 1915. Invalided home the following October, he returned to Egypt in May 1916. Transferred to the Royal Engineers, he is serving as a sapper in Palestine.

ARCHIBALD K. WOOLEY, only son of Alexander Wooley, Invercloy, and manager in the grocery branch of his father's business, offered himself in September 1914, but was not accepted on account of a slight physical defect in his leg. Not to be denied, however, he underwent an operation successfully, and enlisted in the Glasgow Chamber of Commerce Battalion in February 1915. Trained at Troon, etc., he went with the battalion to France in November 1915, and was slightly wounded in the face at the battle of the Somme on 1st July 1916. On recovery, he was transferred to the York and Lancasters, and in October following was severely wounded in the chest and side in an engagement at Le Sars. Conveyed to England, he was in hospital in Stockport, and subsequently in Bolton, until May 1917, when he was transferred to Bellahouston Hospital, Glasgow, being shortly afterwards sent to the convalescent hospital at Lamlash, in which he was an inmate until June 1918, at which date he was sent to clerical work in the orderly room of the 8th York and Lancaster Regiment, Pontefract. During his residence in Lamlash he was much engaged, along with the Marchioness of Graham, promoting concerts throughout the Island, in aid of the Hospital Funds, with great success. Being unfit for further military service, he was discharged from the Army in October 1918, and reverted to his former duties as manager in the business of A. Wooley & Son.

ARCHIE STEWART, younger son of the late John Stewart, Invercloy, employed as clerk at Brodick Pier, attested under the Derby Scheme in December 1915, and was called up in June 1916. Attached to the 12th Battalion, he was trained at Montrose and drafted to France the following October, and served on the Somme and Arras fronts. After a rigorous winter in the trenches, he was invalided home in April 1917, and confined to hospital in Sheffield until February 1918, when he received his discharge. Shortly afterwards he returned to his former duties at Brodick Pier.

JAMES DEWAR, younger son of the late John Dewar (second marriage), head gamekeeper at Brodick Castle, enlisted in June 1916 in the R.F.A. After the usual training at Stobs and Catterick, he went to France in December 1916; was wounded in August 1917, but had been transferred on the field to the 11th Battalion H.L.I.; was sent to the

Highland Light Infantry

Canadian Hospital, Orpington, Kent, from there to Sidcup near London, and then to a convalescent camp in Ireland.

Back to France in December 1917, he was shot through the left wrist in April 1918 and taken to hospital at Boulogne, later to the College Hospital, Didsbury, Manchester. Returning to France in June following, and transferred to the 7th Battalion, he was slightly wounded in the face early in October, but had his wound dressed on the field and never left the battalion.

JOHN SILLARS, Corporal, joiner, employed in the estate workshop at Brodick Castle, eldest son of Robert Sillars, East Knowe, attested under the Derby Scheme, was called up in July 1916 and attached to the Royal Engineers; transferred towards the end of August to the 18th Battalion H.L.I. at Montrose, and in September following sent to the 3rd Battalion, in training at Malleny Camp, near Edinburgh. In January 1917 he was selected to go to the Machine Gun Corps, and sent to Grantham on 3rd February. After being initiated into the mysteries of a Vickers machine-gun in Clipstone Camp, he was in April, after completing his training at Grantham, drafted to France and posted to the 56th (London Territorial) Division, just in time to take part in the final stage of the battle of Arras, 1917. Engaged in the battle of Ypres in August 1917, September found him with the division in the Somme sector, when, after a quiet time, they were

Brodick-Arran and the Great War

subsequently engaged in the battle of Cambrai, which, however, did not prove to be such a great victory as at first believed. In December they went into the Gavrelle sector, and were there during the great German offensive of March 1918. Throughout the following summer they were round about Arras, and later, besides other engagements, at the storming of the Canal du Nord, an important phase of the Cambrai-St Quentin battle. Since joining the division, until hostilities ceased he took part in much hard fighting without injury. Demobilised in February 1919.

PETER ALLISON, employed with Kaspar Ribbeck, Invercloy, was called up on attaining military age on 4th December 1916. Posted to the 12th Battalion, and trained at Kirkcaldy and Dundee, he went to France in April following; was wounded at Ypres on 28th September 1918, and taken to hospital in Norwich, in which he was an inmate for about two months. Demobilised in January 1919.

HENRY RIBBECK, elder son of Adolph Ribbeck, Invercloy, while learning upholstering in Glasgow, was called up on 5th September 1917 on attaining military age, having attested previously. Trained in a training reserve battalion at Kirkcaldy, Kinghorn, and Norwich, he was drafted to France on 2nd April 1918, and joined the 12th Battalion H.L.I. on the Somme. He was later at the Ancre and Ypres, and for about six weeks at a signal training school.

Highland Light Infantry

Having taken part in the advance at Ypres on 28th September, he was on 11th October invalided to England from Dickebusch and taken to Stoke War Hospital, Newcastle, Staffordshire. Demobilised in January 1919.

ERNEST HOPE RIBBECK, elder son of John Ribbeck, Glasgow, and grandson of the late Ernest Ribbeck, Invercloy, was employed in the West of Scotland Insurance Company office, Glasgow, and enlisted in the A.S.C. in June 1917, being afterwards transferred to the 3rd Battalion H.L.I. He was trained at Malleny Camp, and subsequently took up duty at Gailes Camp, where he died of acute pneumonia on 2nd January 1918, aged 19 years. Private Ribbeck was educated at Hillhead High School, and took a great interest in Rugby and other athletics. He was also an active member of Hillhead Boy Scouts, being at the time of his death Assistant Scout Master.

JAMES NICOL, only son of James Nicol, 86 Jamieson Street, Govanhill, Glasgow, and a relative of Archibald Currie, Rowan Bank, Brodick, enlisted in April 1918 on attaining military age. Before enlisting he was a clerk in the office of the Territorial Force Association, West George Street, Glasgow, and for eighteen months an enthusiastic Volunteer in the 3rd Glasgow Battalion, in which he ranked as corporal. Trained at Kelling Camp, Norfolk, he was later at Sherringham, Norfolk, and is now in Germany.

Brodick-Arran and the Great War

Gordon Highlanders

CHARLES HENDRY, a painter, employed on the Arran Estate at Brodick Castle, only son of John Hendry, Glensherrig, attested and was called up on 15th June 1917, on attaining military age. Attached to a training reserve battalion at Tillicoultry, and afterwards in Aberdeen, he was sent to France at the end of March 1918, where he joined the 1/4 Battalion in the 51st Division on the 10th of April, and went into the line near Robecq. Leaving here on 5th May for the Arras front, they set out from this quarter on the 14th of July, and a few days later took up their position in a wood to the left of Rheims. Wounded in this locality on the 20th, by shrapnel in the legs and thigh, he was taken to hospital in Rouen, a few days later to Southampton, thence to the War Hospital in Sunderland. His condition was critical for a time, and he remained in this hospital for ten weeks, when he was sent to a convalescent hospital in Richmond, from there to Sunderland, where he received his discharge from the Army on 29th November.

NEIL CURRIE M'KAY, nephew of Miss Currie, Low Glencloy Cottage, employed with his uncle, Archibald Currie, at Brodick Pier, was called up in September 1917, on attaining military age, having attested previously. After six months' training in Tillicoultry and Cromer, he was sent to France

Seaforth Highlanders

towards the end of March 1918, in the Lewis Gun Section of the 1/7 Battalion, and soon found himself up the line, attached to the famous 51st Division, with which he was engaged in much hard fighting. On duty later in Germany.

Seaforth Highlanders

WILLIAM ALBERT ROBERTSON MONTEITH, 2nd Lieutenant, only son of William Monteith and Elizabeth Robertson Monteith, Sandhurst, Prestwick, Ayrshire, nephew of the Misses Robertson, 29 Keir St., Pollokshields, and Millburn, Lamlash, and closely connected with Brodick on the maternal side, was born in Glasgow on 13th July 1897. Educated at Collegiate and Glasgow Academy, Glasgow, and Ayr Academy, Ayr, he entered the Royal Military College, Sandhurst, in 1916, shortly after leaving school, and obtained his commission in the Seaforth Highlanders in April 1917. In June of same year he proceeded to France, where he served with the 2nd Battalion of his regiment in the 4th Division. · He took part in a number of engagements, the chief of which were Ypres, October 1917; the great German offensive in the spring of 1918; and the Allied advance in autumn following. In the Ypres engagement he was the only officer out of seventeen to get through unwounded. During the German offensive his battalion held the line in the Arras sector successfully against repeated enemy attacks. In the Allied offensive he was severely wounded in the lower part of the body, while gallantly leading his men in an assault on the enemy position, near Eterpigny, on the evening of 31st August. After lying in a shell hole for about four hours, he was brought into the British lines by a brother officer (Jack Aitken) under heavy enemy fire, for which act of gallantry Mr Aitken has been awarded the Military Cross. He was eventually taken to the No. 1 C.C.S. at Ligny St Flochel, where he died on 2nd September, and was buried in the British Military Cemetery there. From the letters of sympathy received by his father from his fellow-officers, it is evident that on account of his bright and cheerful disposition he was a general favourite with both officers and men, and died upholding the best traditions of his regiment.

Royal Berkshire Regiment

JOHN CALDER, Captain, the descendant of a martial race with the blood of the Camerons coursing through his veins, was Free Church minister in Brodick, and being impressed with the righteousness of the war, and the necessity for every able-bodied man throwing himself into the struggle, joined the Inns of Court Officers' Training Corps in November 1914, notwithstanding the prevalent notion that ministers of religion should hold themselves aloof from warfare. Leaving Brodick on New Year's

Royal Berkshire Regiment

Day 1915, he had a most enthusiastic send off, being accompanied by the local pipe band and a large crowd of the inhabitants from the village of Invercloy, where he had been residing, to the pier, where he was cheered again and again as the steamer moved off. Earlier in the day he held a farewell service in the Free Church hall, at which all the denominations in the district were well represented. "The angel of the Lord encampeth round about them that fear Him," was the text of a short sermon, "delivered with restrained emotion and replete with many fine mystic touches." He was trained in London and Berkhamsted, and applied for a commission in the Camerons, the memories of his ancestors' glorious deeds at Culloden, Quebec, and Waterloo acting as a stimulus, but was posted to the Royal Berkshire Regiment, by request of Colonel O. Pearce Serocold, on 26th February 1915. The following month he was ordered to France, and on arrival hurriedly pushed into heavy warfare on the Ypres salient, being in action at Hill 60, the second battle of Ypres, also in minor engagements at Le Gheir, Ploegsteert, and St Ives. Taking over part of the French line at Gommecourt Wood in July, he was that same month appointed Intelligence officer for the battalion, resulting in many stirring adventures in "No-man's-land." Attached to the Staff at Base Headquarters from August to November 1915, he then rejoined his unit and spent the winter in the trenches, the chief work consisting in patrols, raids, etc. In one of these, he and a lance-corporal were cut off by a party of Germans, but escaped in the dark later after an exciting time. He had been appointed second in command of a company, and in May 1916, during furious enemy action, at Hebuterne, had full command of a company. During this action, preceded by three days' enemy bombardment, he was twice buried by high-explosive shells, and later affected by gas shells. Suffering from concussion and gas-poisoning, he was taken to hospital at Rouen, later to Aberdeen, and on recovery joined the reserve battalion in England. In May 1917 he was transferred to the Army Chaplains' Department, and after serving in France as a chaplain with the Camerons and Argylls, was sent to the Salonica British Forces in Greece, under the Foreign Office. He was subsequently attached to the Black Watch in England.

Demobilised in August 1918, he settled down to his ministerial duties in Clachan, Argyllshire, where he had been inducted to the Free Church congregation after severing his connection with Brodick in June 1916.

Lancashire Fusiliers

HARRY BARRETT, stud-groom at Brodick Castle, attested under the Derby Scheme and was called up early in January 1917. Reporting at Stirling, he was sent to the King's Shropshire Light Infantry in England, and subsequently transferred to the Lanca-

1st Bedfords

shire Fusiliers. Landing in France on 26th February he went into the La Bassée sector, and on 24th June left there for Nieuport on the Belgian coast, from which he was shifted to Ypres on 27th September. Early in October he was in an advance of one and a quarter miles at Passchendaele and on 8th January 1918, being hit with shrapnel, he was admitted to hospital with septic poisoning. Leaving the 18th General Hospital at Carmiares, he arrived at Dover on 23rd February, and entered St Luke's Military Hospital, Halifax. Having had his thumb amputated on 12th March, he went later into Scarborough Camp, and receiving his discharge from the Army on 2nd September, he resumed his former duties at Brodick Castle.

1st *Bedfords*

GUY S. G. HAMILTON, Lieutenant and Adjutant, son of Robert C. Hamilton, managing director of the Greenwich Inlaid Linoleum Company in America, having been a non-com. in the O.T.C., Brighton College, the public school in which he was educated, was accepted in December 1914 by the Inns of Court O.T.C. He obtained his commission on 22nd April 1915, and in a month afterwards was fighting with the 1st Bedfords at Hill 60. His service was continuous until April 1917, when he returned to England wounded in the thigh. Passed fit again in July, he was offered two months' light duty, but this he refused in order to return at once to the regiment

Brodick-Arran and the Great War

with which he was then serving—the 8th Battalion Royal West Surreys—of which he was adjutant, a position he reached at the age of 18 years, and I understand he had the honour of being the youngest adjutant in the British Army on active service.

He was unfortunately killed on 1st August by a stray shell at Hill 60, near to the spot where he got his baptism of fire in 1915, at the age of 19½ years, after having been fully two and a half years in the Army.

He was a handsome lad, being 6 feet 1½ inches in height, and every inch a soldier, having evidently inherited the martial spirit from his grandfather on the maternal side, Major Stanley Richer, who was an old campaigner in the British Army, and his uncle, Major F. A. Richer, 15th Hussars.

His connection with Brodick was through his grandfather, the late Gavin Hamilton, Solicitor, Glasgow, a native of the district, and a near relative of Archibald and the Misses Fullarton, Alma, and John and the Misses Allison, Invercloy.

York and Lancaster

MALCOLM KERR, gamekeeper and gardener, Douglas Row, attested under the Derby Scheme in December 1915, and was called to the Colours in January 1917. Reporting at Stirling on the 23rd, he was posted to the Motor Transport Section, and went to Grove Park, London, where he passed the test. In April

Royal Engineers

following he was transferred to the infantry, and put in his training with the 81st Training Reserve Battalion at Gateshead-on-Tyne and Usworth Camp, Durham. Landing in France early in July, he joined the 1/4 York and Lancasters at Etaples, from which they went to Nieuport, where the regiment got badly gassed. Leaving the Belgian coast at the end of September, they went into the sector around Ypres, where the regiment had another bad time. From here he was sent to hospital, sick, on 3rd January 1918, and after being in 54th General Hospital at Wimereux, and the 22nd General Hospital near Etaples, he entered the War Hospital in Bath, England, on 1st April, which he left after three months, and reported at the regimental depot at Pontefract, from which he was sent after a few days to Perkham Down Camp on Salisbury Plain, where he was for five months. Demobilised in January 1919.

Royal Engineers

JOHN CURRIE, Corporal, a joiner to trade, employed in Glasgow, only son of John Currie, Glensherrig, enlisted on 9th April 1915. Trained at Ayr, Catterick, and Codford, he left for France on 20th November, and was for some time located about Albert, afterwards at the Somme in July 1916. Later about St Quentin, from which he was moved to Nieuport, where he was wounded on the foot and slightly gassed on 19th July 1917. While constructing a bridge in this quarter, the engineers were under heavy enemy fire and the bridge swept away five times in succession before the task was accomplished. From Nieuport he was admitted into Edmonton Hospital, London, on 24th July, and three weeks later transferred to a convalescent hospital. After sick leave he reported at Thetford on 22nd September, which he left for Newark on 24th November, and went into hospital there on 1st March 1918, suffering with his eyes from the effects of gas-poisoning. He left again for France on 15th August 1918, and while at the base was sent to hospital at Rouen on 14th December; removed later to Trouville. Demobilised in February 1919.

JAMES NICOL, only son of the late James Nicol, Douglas Row, employed in Kilmarnock, enlisted early, and after being in France for a long time, was wounded in the left arm in the beginning of September 1918 and conveyed to Lichfield Hospital. He was engaged in the later stage of the South African War.

JOHN K. CAMERON MORRISON, Sapper, youngest son of the late Angus Morrison, Douglas Row, is a joiner to trade. He was in Canada for a few years, and coming home after the war had commenced, enlisted on 7th June 1915. Trained at Scotstoun and Kilwinning, he crossed to France in the end of September 1916. Landing at Rouen, he was after a short spell there posted to the 400th Field

Royal Engineers

Company, attached to the 51st Division, in the Somme. Leaving here in January 1917, they were later engaged in the battle of Arras, moving subsequently to the Ypres salient and taking part in the offensive there, afterwards to the Cambrai front, where the Sapper was gassed in February 1918 and taken to an American Red Cross Hospital at Paignton, in Devonshire. On recovery, and after about six months on home duty, he left again for France in the end of September and joined the 404th Field Company, with the 51st Division, in the vicinity of Valenciennes, where he continued up to the time of the Armistice, being ultimately demobilised in February 1919.

ALEXANDER KENNEDY, Sapper, only son of John Alexander Kennedy, bootmaker, Greenock, and grandson of the late Captain William Inglis of Brodick and Greenock, joined the Colours on 29th November 1915, and was posted to the Royal Engineers.

Trained at Stanecastle, Irvine, most of his service was spent on A. A. work in Scotland and England, including a short spell in London.

Before enlisting he was employed in the commercial department of Scotts' Shipbuilding and Engineering Co., Ltd., Greenock, and returned to his duties there, after demobilisation, on 13th January 1919. He is a near relative of the writer.

DAVID ALLAN, Sapper, second son of William

Brodick-Arran and the Great War

Allan, West Knowe, was gardener to Sir Matthew Nathan, manager of Nobel's explosive factory at Ardeer, and assisted at the loading of the ammunition wagons after the outbreak of war until February 1916, when he enlisted. Completing his training at Chatham, he was drafted to France early in November and attached to the 26th Field Company, later to the 233rd Field Company. Subsequently engaged in the fighting at the sand dunes in Belgium, and at the Somme, he was slightly wounded at La Bassée in the spring of 1918, and again slightly wounded by shrapnel on the back at St Quentin on 28th September 1918.

WILLIAM M'AUSLAN, Sapper, younger son of David M'Auslan, Douglas Row, late head gardener at Brodick Castle, who learned engineering at the Power Station, Brodick Castle, and afterwards employed in Beardmore's Works, Dalmuir, was called up in July 1917, and sent to France in January 1918 from Dover, where he had been trained.

King's Own Scottish Borderers

PETER C. W. RIBBECK, only son of Donald Ribbeck, Glasgow, and grandson of the late Ernest Ribbeck, Invercloy, enlisted on attaining military age in May 1918, in the 4th Battalion.

Trained at Dunfermline and Ladybank, he was about to enter the Air Force as a cadet, having

Royal Army Medical Corps

passed his examination and awaiting instructions to proceed to England, when hostilities ceased. Is now on duty in Cologne.

Royal Army Medical Corps

WILLIAM M'KAY, Sergeant, nephew of Miss Currie, Low Glencloy Cottage, was an employee of the Glasgow Corporation with a view to become a sanitary inspector, and joined the Territorials at the age of 16. Called up on the declaration of war at the age of 17, and sent to Falkirk, he was, at the age of 18, made a sergeant, and kept in Britain training others until August 1917, when he was drafted to Egypt, and in October 1918 was still there in the 1/1 Welsh Field Ambulance with the 53rd Division.

Royal Field Artillery

ALEXANDER WATT, Corporal, only son of Alexander Watt, Glasgow, and nephew of Mrs Archibald Sillars, Kilmichael, and of Archibald Currie, Brodick Pier, was for two years an apprentice iron turner in Glasgow, when he decided to enlist as a regular soldier, a life which had always appealed to him. Enlisting at Glasgow Cross on 15th January 1913, he underwent recruit training at Maryhill Barracks, and was posted as a gunner to the 13th Battery, 7th Brigade, then stationed at Piershill Barracks Edin-

Brodick-Arran and the Great War

burgh. Promoted to the rank of bombardier in July 1914 at Buddon Camp, near Dundee, where his brigade were doing the duties of training brigade to batteries of the Territorial Force, it was at this camp that orders were received to mobilise, and within sixteen hours they were back in barracks in Edinburgh. After three days' stay there the personnel alone of the brigade left for Aldershot, and were given a rousing send off by the people of " Auld Reekie." The men of the 13th Battery, brought up to full strength by reservists, formed the brigade ammunition column of the 34th Brigade. Going out to France as a signaller and mounted ammunition orderly, he landed with the brigade at Boulogne on 17th August 1914. After twenty-four hours' rest they entrained for the front, and detraining at Wassigny on the 20th, marched for three days and dropped into action against the enemy on Sunday afternoon of the 23rd in the memorable battle of Mons, when "the contemptible little army" had to face such tremendous odds. After a struggle lasting twenty-four hours, the great retreat commenced through France towards Paris, which terminated at the Marne. This gallant warrior took part in all the principal fighting, from Mons to shortly before the great German offensive in March 1918, when he was forced to leave his unit, and subsequently underwent an operation for appendicitis in St Louis American Hospital, Rouen. Taken to Sploit Road Military Hospital, Cardiff, he was sent convalescent, about the beginning of April, to St John's Hospital,

Royal Field Artillery

Barry Island, near Cardiff, which he left on 23rd April, and reported on 3rd May at the Command Depot, Ripon, Yorks. From this centre he was discharged medically unfit for further service on 26th August 1918, after having been in the Army for fully five and a half years, of which three years and seven months were spent on active service in many memorable engagements along the whole British front—at Ypres, Neuve Chapelle, Festubert, La Bassée, Loos, Vimy Ridge, the Somme, the Ancre, Arras, Messines, Cambrai, etc.

DONALD M'COLL, Corporal Saddler, Argyll and Bute Mounted Battery (Territorial), a saddler with Henry Ribbeck, Invercloy, was mobilised immediately after the declaration of war. Leaving Brodick on 5th August 1914, he embarked on 17th March 1915 with the 29th Division for Gallipoli, after training in Bedford. Landing at Alexandria on 1st April, they were inspected by Sir Ian Hamilton and the French Commander-in-Chief, sailing four days later for Lemnos Harbour, where they underwent very heavy training, climbing up and down the side of the ship in full fighting order, preparing for the landing at Cape Helles, where they arrived on the morning of 25th April, with the sun rising in all its splendour. But another and awful splendour was just to begin. With the booming of the guns of the Fleet bombarding the Turkish forts and trenches and covering the landing, the noise was terrible, and it was very trying indeed on the nerves to see boat-loads of the most gallant fellows getting killed by the enemy before reaching land. After the infantry had got a firm grip on the shore, the guns were ordered to be landed, and the Corporal has the impression that the 4th Highland Battery had the honour of being the first artillery to land on the peninsula.

They were ultimately withdrawn from Cape Helles and landed on Imbros Island, from which they embarked for the landing at Suvla Bay, which was accomplished fairly easy, with every prospect of a great success; but it, however, eventually proved a failure, and they in consequence suffered many privations.

While the evacuation was taking place, it fell to their lot to cover the retreat. Getting off all the extra ponies, and only having enough for the guns, they got orders that these were to be shot when the guns were taken to the beach; but this was going to be a painful job, and they somehow or other got a barge and managed to save the Highland ponies, though the guns were lost in transit. Taken to Egypt, the battery was equipped with new guns, and after a few bouts with the enemy in the desert they embarked for Salonica, where Corporal M'Coll was subsequently in hospital for several months with malaria. On rejoining his unit he took part in the fighting in that region, and having been again invalided to hospital with influenza, he was ultimately sent to England towards the end of 1918 and subsequently discharged.

Royal Field Artillery

ALEXANDER WOOLEY, son of Donald Wooley, blacksmith, Braco, Perthshire, and nephew of Alexander Wooley, Invercloy, enlisted on 5th September 1914. Trained at Redford Barracks, Colinton, Edinburgh, he went to France on 23rd October 1915, and served on the Somme, Arras, and Ypres fronts. Invalided in June 1918, he was taken to Northumberland War Hospital, Newcastle-on-Tyne. Demobilised 28th January 1919.

JAMES C. DAVIDSON, Driver, second son of the late Robert Davidson, Glenrosa, was employed working the farm when he intimated to the recruiting officers in the early summer of 1915 his willingness to join the Forces when the harvest was secured. Accordingly, in October 1915 he was called to the Colours, and after training in Rothesay for a month or two, was transferred to Richmond, from which he was dispatched to France after six months' training altogether.

Engaged in the ammunition column of the R.F.A., he was constantly with the famous 51st Division, and shared the hardships of the retreat resulting from the great German offensive of 21st March 1918. Although they had to leave many of their guns behind in the indescribable tumult, they were soon fully equipped again with new ones from Albert, and afterwards engaged stemming the advance at Robecq when the Portuguese were forced back. He was in engagements at Ypres, Arras, the Somme, Beaumont Hamel, the Marne, and other parts, and got through without injury. Demobilised in February 1919.

DUNCAN M'INTYRE, Gunner, brother of Mrs Kelly, Douglas Row, had been in the employment of the forestry department at Brodick Castle, and like his brother, Corporal Duncan M'Intyre, was, at the outbreak of war, a gardener with Mr Kirkpatrick, Coupar-Angus, Whiting Bay. He enlisted in December 1915, was trained at Redford Barracks, Edinburgh, and embarked for France on 25th June 1916. Engaged in the battle of the Somme, 1st July 1916, he was wounded on the right shoulder and ribs on 25th August, at Delville Wood. Taken to the 6th Scottish Hospital at Rouen, he was later sent to Cambuslang Hospital, Glasgow. Embarking again for France on 22nd December 1916, he took part in much fighting, and was wounded in the left arm and neck at Ypres on 31st July 1917. Wounded again at Passchendaele in the lower part of the body on 14th November 1917, he was conveyed to hospital in Sheffield, and on 1st October 1918 received his discharge from the Army at the 4th General Scottish Hospital, Stobhill, Glasgow. He served with B Battery, 70th Brigade, and D Battery, 86th Brigade.

DUNCAN BRUCE, Gunner, second son of John Bruce, Sannox, and nephew of Mrs Dugald Langlands, Invercloy, employed with Kaspar Ribbeck, Invercloy, as motor driver, attested under the Derby Scheme in December 1915, was called up in March

Royal Field Artillery

1916; trained in Edinburgh, and only a short time in France when he was killed on 17th November 1916.

JOHN HAMILTON, Gunner, eldest son of Lachlan Hamilton, Dhunan, employed on his father's farm, enlisted in August 1916. Trained in Edinburgh, he was sent to France in December 1916 and wounded in the left arm and shoulder in June 1917. For about six weeks in the 4th London Hospital, he was then removed to Stobhill Hospital, Glasgow, and after being in a convalescent hospital in Wigtownshire and Aberdeen, was discharged unfit for further service in December 1917. Fortunately he is not wholly incapacitated for work in civil life, and is now working on the farm.

WILLIAM M'NICOL, Gunner, an apprentice plumber at Brodick Castle, eldest son of Colin M'Nicol, Douglas Row, was called up after attesting, on attaining military age, on 14th March 1917. After training in Edinburgh, he was transferred to the Tank Corps in July 1917 and sent to Bovington for further training, thence to France 25th December following. He was wounded in the arm and legs in the end of September 1918 and treated in hospital in France, joining his unit, the 11th Battalion, about the end of October. He served on the Somme, La Bassée, Arras and Cambrian fronts. Demobilised in January 1919.

WILLIAM R. HAMILTON, employed with Duncan M'Arthur, Merkland, was called to the Colours in

Brodick-Arran and the Great War

December 1917, on reaching military age. He proceeded to Stirling, thence to Redford Barracks, Edinburgh, and from there to Bettesfield Camp, Whitchurch, Salop, where he went through a course of training qualifying him as a signaller, and later located at Crowbridge, Sussex.

ARCHIBALD F. SILLARS, Driver, eldest son of Archibald Sillars, Kilmichael, volunteered in July 1915, but was rejected owing to a strained heart. Attesting under the Derby Scheme, he was classed C 3. He was called up under the Military Act in January 1918, and passed A 1. For a few days in Redford Barracks, Edinburgh, he was sent on for training to Bettesfield Camp, Whitchurch, Salop, and in June embarked for France, where he was selected to undergo a course of training to fulfil the duties of a signaller, and later went up the line, where he joined the 122nd Brigade, 38th Division.

Previous to enlisting, he was on the staff of the Conservative Club, Glasgow.

GUY B. ROBERTSON, Lieutenant, son of the Right Honourable John MacKinnon Robertson, Parliamentary Secretary to the Board of Trade in the Asquith Administration previous to the formation of the Coalition, was commissioned on 29th January 1915; went overseas on 19th November 1915; wounded in September 1916; slightly gassed in July 1917; and promoted lieutenant in December following. He has a close connection with Brodick, his father being a native of the district and a near relative of Miss MacKinnon, Low Glencloy.

Royal Garrison Artillery

THOMAS WALKER, Gunner, elder son of William Walker, shoemaker, Invercloy, a shoemaker to trade assisting his father in the business, attested under the Derby Scheme and was exempted several times, but called up finally in March 1917. Passing the educational test at Plymouth Citadel on 18th March, he was sent to Chatham Signalling Depot, where he obtained a first-class certificate for signalling and telephony on 20th September 1917. Drafted to Catterick, Yorkshire, for more advanced training, he also obtained a first-class certificate for signalling and telephony on 12th October.

Embarking at Southampton on 13th December on the well-known Caledonian Company's steamer *Duchess of Argyle*, the draft landed at Le Havre the same evening. There being a scarcity of bootmakers in the Army, he was chosen to work at his trade, and for a time had charge of one of the base workshops until a demand was made for men up the line, when he was appointed to the 46th Siege Battery, which he joined at Feuchy in the Scarpe Valley. Since then his duties varied very much.

Previous to the opening of the German offensive, the battery retired to a position at St Nicolas, a suburb of Arras, where they did excellent work in

Brodick-Arran and the Great War

the battle of Arras on the morning of 28th March, for which they were complimented by the General Commanding. No one, Gunner Walker says, can realise the great strain it is on men, the moving of heavy artillery in a retreat. The battery had to fall back a few miles again and ordered to stand by, this movement being covered by a battery of six howitzers. Returning to the same position four days afterwards, the battery remained there until the end of April, when it was relieved by a Canadian battery.

Ordered to take up position at Anzin, which they held until the end of August, they then got orders to move forward again to position on Bailleul Road to assist in clearing the enemy out of Monchy, Fampoux, and neighbouring positions. When the enemy was pushed back from Monchy, this battery got orders to pull out and stand by, finally getting orders to take up positions on Arras-Cambrai road, where it was when Gunner Walker went on leave early in October. He was later at Mons. Demobilised in February 1919.

CHARLES RIBBECK, Gunner, fourth son of Henry Ribbeck, senior, Invercloy, foreman cutter with Messrs Robert Hunter & Son, tailors, St Vincent Street, Glasgow, attested under the Derby Scheme but was exempted until 18th April 1918, when he was called up and underwent training in No. 3 Battery, 3rd S.A.R.B., at Winchester and Prees Heath Camp, Whitchurch. Demobilised in February 1919.

Royal Air Force

Royal Air Force

JOHN ALLAN, Chief Mechanic, eldest son of William Allan, West Knowe, was a joiner on the Arran estate at Brodick Castle and attested under the Derby Scheme in December 1915. Called up in July 1916, he was posted to the Royal Engineers, but shortly afterwards transferred to the Air Force at Drighton, Shropshire, later to Stockbridge, Hants. Demobilised in February 1919.

ALLAN RIBBECK, youngest son of Henry Ribbeck, senior, Invercloy, a watchmaker to trade, carrying on business in Dumbarton, attested under the Derby Scheme and was called up in July 1916. Sent on to Farnborough, he was employed there as a 2nd air mechanic and drafted to Italy in November following. Demobilised in March 1919.

VICTOR SILLARS, Lieutenant, eldest son of John Sillars, West Mayish, assisted his father on the farm. Having been exempted for some time after attaining to military age, he was called up in June 1917 and sent to Farnborough, afterwards transferred to St Leonards-on-Sea. Passing the Medical Air Board at Hotel Cecil as fit for a pilot in the beginning of September, he went to the School of Aeronautics about the middle of that month and passed his final examination on 13th November. Receiving his

Brodick-Arran and the Great War

commission on the 16th, he was sent on the 26th to Waddington, Lincoln, for flying, and had his first flight on 6th December. Graduating on 18th March 1918, and promoted to 1st lieutenant in April, he flew to France on 13th June, and shot down his first two enemy machines on 7th July after an exciting encounter at an altitude of 15,000 feet. Three British machines were lost against seven enemy ones and two enemy ones driven down out of control. The battle, he says, was fast and furious, and the enemy were out-manœuvred, out-sailed, and out-fought from the outset. He had bad luck to begin with, and was nearly knocked out by a shot through the inlet pipe of his rear carburettor. No sooner had the enemy seen his crippled condition than they swooped down on him, and two at least made the attack. Within a short time, however, both were hurtling earthwards riddled with bullets, the gallant lieutenant manœuvring the machine while his illustrious observer played the gun on them with deadly accuracy.

COSIMO LATONA, apprentice engineer with the Albion Motor Company, Glasgow, eldest son of Cosimo Latona, Brodick, enlisted on 12th December 1917, and was sent to Aldershot, later to Shawbury, near Shrewsbury, where he is a 2nd air mechanic.

ALEXANDER SILLARS, fifth son of Robert Sillars, East Knowe, was learning motor engineering in Glasgow when called up in the spring of 1918 and

Army Service Corps

dispatched to England; now stationed at Edmonton as a 2nd air mechanic.

ROBERT DAVIDSON, an engineer to trade, working on the Clyde, fifth son of the late Robert Davidson, Glenrosa, enlisted in the Black Watch in July 1918, but was transferred, on account of his trade, to the Flying Corps. After a short spell in England, he proceeded to Malta in September, and was stationed later on the island of Thasos and at Mudros.

Army Service Corps

DUNCAN LANGLANDS, Corporal, Douglas Row, engaged in the forestry department at Brodick Castle, enlisted in October 1914, but was not accepted for the Lovat Scouts. However, he again offered himself successfully in December 1915, and was posted to the A.S.C. He was on duty in England, and demobilised in February 1919.

JOHN PATERSON, Staff - Sergeant Saddler, a saddler with Henry Ribbeck, Invercloy, was at Aldershot and thereabout until March 1916, when he was sent to Salonica, where he is still serving.

NEIL SHAW, only son of Neil Shaw, Commercial Hotel, Portpatrick, and grandson of the late Robert

Brodick-Arran and the Great War

Shaw, Douglas Row, Brodick, was one of the northern travellers located in Dundee of the firm of Hamilton Brothers, provision merchants, Wilson Street, Glasgow. Born in Glasgow and educated in Shawlands Academy and Hutchison Boys' School, he enlisted in February 1915, and having a practical knowledge of the baking trade, was posted to the 16th Field Bakery, A.S.C. Trained at Fermoy, Ireland, and Blackdown Camp, England, he crossed to France in December 1915. Having studied at the Technical College, Glasgow, to learn fermentation, and with a knowledge of chemistry, for which he held two first-class diplomas, he was regularly employed in the laboratory. Hard luck now awaited him. Getting the usual home leave, he was recalled at Calais on board the transport, on 23rd March 1918, to rejoin his unit. Transferred to the 11th Cheshires on 13th April, as the pressure for men in the fighting line was then great, he was unfortunately killed on 3rd May following, and buried at Locre. He was an excellent golfer, for which he won many prizes, and during his holidays in Brodick was well known on the golf course.

WILLIAM FREDERICK HILL, only son of William Hill, Partick, and grandson of the late James Houliston, Glensherrig, Brodick, enlisted in January 1916. A fortnight afterwards he was sent to France, and after fifteen months there was transferred to a Welsh regiment in Aldershot, where he underwent a short training. Returning to France, he was gassed

Motor Transport

and lost his voice for some time. He was a butcher before enlisting.

ANGUS SMITH, Driver, youngest son of Archibald Smith, Douglas Row, employed at wood-cutting in Perthshire, enlisted early in 1916, and was for a spell in England before being sent to France in February 1917.

Motor Transport

NEIL SILLARS, Driver, employed as motor driver with Mr Laidler, factor, Strabane, third son of Robert Sillars, East Knowe, attested under the Derby Scheme, joined the Motor Transport Section in January 1916, and four weeks later landed in France, and has served on all parts of the British front. He was with the 42nd Siege Battery when hostilities ceased.

WILLIAM KERR, Driver, Invercloy, employed with Dr Jamieson, Glencloy, as motor driver and gardener, fifth son of the late Alexander Kerr, Dunfion, attested under the Derby Scheme and was called up in June 1916. Trained principally at Aldershot, he landed in France on 11th November 1916, and was engaged carrying ammunition to the 192nd Siege Battery at Loos, Ypres, Vimy, Arras, Amiens, etc., and near Cambrai when the Armistice was signed.

Brodick-Arran and the Great War

Motor Machine Gun Corps

JOHN M'KAY, elder son of James M'Kay, Edinburgh, and grandson of the late James Houliston, Glensherrig, Brodick, enlisted in April 1915 and went to Bisley. After six months' training he was sent to France and did some dispatch work at the battle of Loos. Transferred subsequently to Egypt, he was in action in the desert and was afterwards engaged fighting with the Arabs against the Turks in the Red Sea Littoral.

In civil life he was a foreman in a large seed warehouse in Leith.

Canadians

JOHN M'INTYRE, eldest son of William M'Intyre, Douglas Row, enlisted in the 79th Cameron Highlanders on 13th August 1914, at Winnipeg, where he was book-keeper in the wholesale dry goods firm of Messrs Robinson, Little, & Co.

He went into Valcartier Camp, Quebec, on the 27th, and left for England two days later on board the S.S. *Andania* of the Cunard Company, one of a large fleet of vessels laden with troops, arriving at their destination on 14th October. Camped and trained principally on Salisbury Plain, he embarked with his unit at Avonmouth for France on 10th

Canadians

February 1915, arriving at St Nazaire three days later, from which they proceeded to Hazebrouck. His first experience of actual warfare was on 24th February, when the Canadians went into the trenches on the Armentières front, along with the Argyll and Sutherland Highlanders.

Moved to the Ypres sector on 20th April, he was slightly wounded on the top of the head by a machine-gun bullet on the 22nd, but able for active duty again in a few days. From that time down to 8th August 1918 he was engaged on all parts of the British front from Belgium to the Somme, and took part in much hard fighting at Ypres, Arras, Vimy Ridge, etc. Wounded severely in the chest by machine-gun bullet again on the aforesaid date, he was conveyed to hospital in Epsom, England, from which he was discharged convalescent towards the end of November. He was altogether forty-two months on active service, and served in the 16th Canadian Scottish, to which his unit had been drafted.

GEORGE GUTHRIE, Sapper, Alberta, son-in-law of Dugald Langlands, Invercloy, employed as a civil engineer with the Canadian Northern Railway Company, enlisted on 23rd January 1915 in the 49th Edmonton Regiment, arrived in England 26th September 1915. Located at Shorncliffe, he was dispatched to France on 3rd October 1915. On 16th September 1916 he was wounded in the left groin and taken to Middlesex War Hospital, St Albans, London. He was subsequently doing

Brodick-Arran and the Great War

clerical work at the Canadian General Hospital, Kent.

JOHN M'NAUGHTON, Sergeant, nephew of Malcolm Gillies, Glenriggart, was at farming in Canada, and enlisted at Edmonton on 5th February 1915, in the 51st Battalion Canadians. After training at Edmonton and Sarcee, he landed at Plymouth about 22nd September and went into camp at Shorncliffe, where he had been transferred to the 49th Battalion before proceeding to France on 9th October. Landing at Boulogne, he was a few days later in the fighting line at Ploegsteert, and subsequently served on various parts of the British front, among them being Kemmel, Hooge, Ypres, the Somme, Vimy Ridge, Arras, Cambrai, Amiens, and was near Mons when hostilities ceased. He has taken part in many engagements, and was once slightly wounded, in the Albert sector, on 15th September 1916.

For about six months he was a drill instructor at Ferfay School, France. He visited the old home in Glenriggart several times on leave.

WILLIAM HAY, Corporal, nephew of Alexander Wooley, Invercloy, joined the British Columbian Horse in the summer of 1915, and transferred to the Canadian Artillery in November of that year. Stationed at Esquimalt for training, he left Victoria, B.C., on 10th December for overseas, completing his training at Shorncliffe, England, on 1st April 1916, when he went to France.

Canadians

WILLIAM WATSON, Corporal, youngest son of John Watson, Vancouver, late of Glencloy Farm, Brodick, arrived in England about the end of 1915, and after a few months' training was sent to France, and engaged at the taking of Vimy Ridge in April 1917. He was wounded in August 1917, and killed in November or December following. While on leave, he visited Brodick and the old home.

WILLIAM KELSO, Corporal Piper, second son of James Kelso, Alma Terrace, for many years an architect in Glasgow, later in Montreal, enlisted in the Canadian Royal Highlanders, and has been for a very considerable time in France in the 13th Battalion Canadians.

GEORGE LANGLANDS, nephew of Dugald Langlands, Invercloy, was employed in the forestry department at Brodick Castle before going to Canada, where he enlisted in March 1916 in a forestry company, and left for France in October following.

JOHN M'DONALD, Lieutenant, grandson of Mrs M'Donald, Invercloy, eldest son of James M'Donald, Lacombe nurseries, Alberta, enlisted in the 151st Central Alberta Regiment on 20th December 1915. Arriving in England on 30th October 1916, and located in Shorncliffe, Kent, he crossed to France on 13th November following, attached to the 78th

Brodick-Arran and the Great War

Battalion. On 15th November 1917 he returned to England to train for a commission, and having studied at the Canadian Training School, Brixhill-on-Sea, Sussex, he was, on 26th January 1918, appointed a lieutenant in the 78th Winnipeg Grenadiers (Canadian Guards), and crossed to France again on 13th March 1918. Engaged at Amiens on 8th August, he received a compound fracture of the left forearm and was taken to the War Hospital, Exeter, Devon. By the middle of October he was again fit for general service, and returned to France early in November.

He had been engaged at Vimy Ridge, Amiens, and other battles, and was awarded the Military Cross for gallantry at Amiens.

JAMES HAMILTON, second son of Lachlan Hamilton, Dhunan, was at farming in Canada, and enlisted on 28th February 1916 in the Lethbridge Highlanders, Alberta, drafted later to the 16th Canadian Scottish. Trained at Calgary, he landed in England early in September, and after further training in Kent crossed to France about the middle of November. Engaged at the taking of Vimy Ridge on 9th April 1917, he was wounded through the left thigh. Taken to a Red Cross Hospital in France, thence to Aldershot, later to a convalescent hospital and depot, and then to the Reserve Battalion at Shorncliffe, from which he was dispatched to France again on 7th April 1918, rejoining his battalion later on the Arras front. From this they went to Amiens, where they

Canadians

were located from the 8th to the 25th August, and returned after a good deal of fighting to Arras. Here he was wounded with shrapnel on the right arm and left hip on 2nd September. Having had his arm amputated, he was taken to hospital near Boulogne, afterwards to 1st Southern General Hospital, Birmingham, and later to the Canadian Special Hospital at Buxton. He visited Brodick early in December, on the eve of sailing for Canada.

GEORGE HENDERSON, Corporal, building contractor, Edmonton, son-in-law of Donald Henderson, Birchvale, Brodick, joined the Canadian A.M.C. in Edmonton in December 1916. Landing in England in March 1917, he was located in Surrey until sent to France in February 1918.

DAVID M'DONALD, Lance-Corporal, younger brother of the aforesaid Lieutenant John M'Donald, enlisted in the 191st Canadian Overseas Battalion at Red Deer, Alberta. He arrived in England in April 1917, and was located in Bramshott Camp, Hampshire, returning to America about 20th November 1918.

During his residence in England he was in a young soldiers' battalion, not having attained to full military age.

Brodick-Arran and the Great War

Australians

JAMES FINLAY TAYLOR, 29th Battalion Australian Imperial Force, only son of James Taylor, retired Glasgow merchant, Strathwhillan, was settled in Melbourne prior to the war, and offered himself for active service in October 1914, but rejected, as he was slightly under the Australian regulation height, which, however, at that time was considerably above the British standard. On the standard being lowered he at once joined the Colours, and went into training on 1st July 1915. He served in Egypt, then in France, and was severely wounded at Bapaume on 1st March 1917. For six months an inmate of East Dulwich Military Hospital, afterwards in Southall Australian Auxiliary Hospital, then classed B 2 B in Weymouth in October; shipped for Melbourne on 4th November, and there discharged on 9th March 1918, but still attending hospital daily for treatment.

ARCHIE WOOLEY, second son of Charles Wooley, harbour-master, Fiji, and nephew of Alexander Wooley, Invercloy, was in the Australian Royal Engineers, but joined the infantry after war broke out. He took part in the Gallipoli campaign, and was slightly wounded; subsequently in Egypt, he is still in the Eastern war front. It may be of interest to note that he was being conveyed to the war zone when the *Sydney* of the Australian Fleet encountered

Australians

and destroyed the enemy raider *Emden* at Cocos Island.

PETER MACKINNON, third son of the late James MacKinnon, Orbost, East Gippsland, Victoria, late of Strathwhillan, Brodick, enlisted in the 8th Battalion Australian Imperial Force in July 1915. Trained at Seymour Camp, Melbourne, he landed at Port Said on 1st January 1916, thence to France in March 1916, and killed in action at Pozières on 25th July 1916.

DONALD BROWN NICOL, second son of the late Archibald Nicol, Buli, New South Wales, and nephew of Alexander, Archibald and Miss Brown, Invercloy, was employed in the Telegraph Department of Sydney Post Office, and a member of the Australian Cadet Corps. On reaching the age of 19 he joined the Australian Imperial Forces, and was in training in Australia for six months. Arriving in England early in November 1916, he was located in Hurdcott Camp, Salisbury Plain, with the 56th Battalion. While there he developed appendicitis, for which he underwent a successful operation. Drafted to France in April 1917, he took part in the trench warfare in the vicinity of Ypres. On being relieved from the trenches on the 15th October, he was wounded by the explosion of a German shell, and died the same night at the field dressing station and buried in the Military Cemetery at Poperinghe. He seems to have had a presentiment previously, for his sergeant, writing to his friends, says, " I might tell you that young Don had a presentiment just previous to getting his wound. He said, ' Even if I lose the left arm I could still carry on at my profession,' so wasn't it strange that he should get hit on both these limbs."

CHARLES WOOLEY, eldest son of the aforesaid Charles Wooley, Fiji, and son-in-law of Neil Crawford, Alma Terrace, is an engineer to trade, and arrived in England in June 1916. After visiting his uncle at Invercloy, he was employed in Government work by Messrs G. & J. Weir, Cathcart, Glasgow. In May 1917 he joined the I.W.T. Branch, Royal Engineers, and became an engineer on board the dredger *Riparian*, engaged keeping channels open across the Goodwin Sands. Demobilised in February 1919.

ALEXANDER G. MACKINNON, 6th Battalion Australian Imperial Force, eldest son of the late James MacKinnon, Orbost, and brother of the aforesaid Peter MacKinnon, enlisted on 25th May 1917. Sailing from Melbourne on 4th August via Panama, he landed off the transport at Glasgow on 2nd October, and was conveyed to Sutton Veny camp, Wilts, England, where he continued training until 2nd April 1918, when he was drafted to France. Wounded on 23rd August 1918, he was sent to hospital in Exeter, Devonshire, afterwards to a convalescent camp at Tiverton, and by the end of

Australians

October, was back in camp at Sutton Veny, fit for service again.

DONALD WOOLEY, third son of Charles Wooley, Fiji, landed in England with a contingent from Fiji, via Panama, on 14th August 1918, and was attached to the King's Royal Rifles at Sheerness.

ROBERT F. INGLIS, Gunner, second son of John Inglis, Hobart, Tasmania, and nephew of William, James C., and Miss Inglis, Invercloy, enlisted in October 1917. He was an apprentice engineer in Hobart, and in the Australian Naval Reserve. In November he entered Claremont Camp, Tasmania, for training in the 27th Reinforcements of the 12th Battalion, and during his stay there, was swimming instructor to the new recruits. Transferred to a wireless corps in January 1918, he was shifted to Moorepark Camp, Sydney, and while there, was attached for a short time to the Australian Light Horse. By the middle of June he was transferred to the 9th N.S.W. General Service Reinforcements at Liverpool Camp, and on the 19th June embarked on H.M.S. *Field Marshal*, a captured German steamer, and left Sydney for England the same day, calling at Albany, Durban, Cape Town, and Sierra Leone, where convoy was picked up, arriving at the Royal Docks, London, on 25th August after an uneventful voyage so far as submarines were concerned, none of these pests having been seen. From London they were conveyed to Codford Camp

Brodick-Arran and the Great War

Salisbury Plain, and transferred to the 55th Battalion. After three weeks they were removed to Hurdcott Camp, and after three more weeks he was transferred to the R.B.A.A. at Heytesbury Camp. He went to France in the end of November. Owing to his naval training, he was selected as a signalman on the voyage to England. Like the other Australian lads, he visited Brodick and his relatives there.

WILLIAM INGLIS, a clerk in the office of the M.A.P.S. in Hobart, eldest son of the aforesaid John Inglis, and nephew of William, James C., and Miss Inglis, Invercloy, enlisted in December 1917, after several unsuccessful attempts due to the effects of a serious operation for appendicitis a couple of years previously. Trained in Claremont Camp, Tasmania, for about three months, he left in April for Sydney, and embarked there for Egypt in the S.S. *Port Darwin* at the end of that month. Calling at Fremantle, W.A., and Colombo, the contingent disembarked at Suez early in June, and went into camp at Ismailia, where he completed his training with a course of equitation. He is in the A.S.C., attached to the Anzac Mounted Division, and was with the Division in Palestine when hostilities ceased.

This young Colonial soldier has shown very great powers of observation, as well as a clear and graphic way of expressing what he has seen. His experiences in the Holy Land are particularly interesting, and naturally and vividly told in letters to his

Australians

relatives in this country. Besides those very realistic descriptive passages in his letters, there are interesting personal notes of Arran men who strangely enough were serving in his own brigade.

He tells how, on one occasion, after the assault on Ammon, when a body of Turks in the hills desired to surrender to the British Forces under the white flag, a party under a Colonial officer was sent out to bring them in. With typical Turkish perfidy the Turks suddenly opened fire on the Colonials, killing the officer and one man, while the others were wounded. Another party of the Australians on scouting duty, observing this act of dastardly treachery, charged the Turks and rode them down to death, a fitting end to their infamous behaviour.

The officer who was so treacherously done to death was Lieutenant ARCHIBALD CURRIE, a son of the late Peter Currie, Glenlaog, Arran. He enlisted in the Australian Light Horse at the commencement of the war along with JAMES INGLIS SWEET, a son of John B. Sweet, banker, Lamlash, both of whom were engaged on Wellshot Sheep Station, Queensland, and after serving in Gallipoli he was promoted to the rank of lieutenant. He was a competent and dashing Colonial soldier. It is interesting to Arran people to know that they have been represented in the illustrious Anzac Corps which has won immortal glory in Gallipoli, Egypt, and in the land of Palestine.

Brodick-Arran and the Great War

South Africans

CHARLES WAKEFORD, son of George Wakeford, Mayor of Barkly West, was engaged throughout the South-West African campaign. He is closely connected with Brodick, his mother, Katie Brown, being a daughter of the late Neil Brown, Invercloy, and a near relative of Alexander, Archibald, and Miss Brown, Mrs D. Smith, and the Misses Currie, Invercloy.

On the successful termination of hostilities in South-West Africa, he was bent on coming to the European Western front, but was prevented by illness contracted in that campaign.

On recovery, however, the desire was still so strong that he sailed for England in June 1918, with a view to serve in the field or in any other capacity that his services might be required.

P. C. RICHARDS, Lieutenant, Town Clerk of Barkly West, husband of Katie Brown MacCauly, grand-daughter of the aforesaid late Neil Brown, volunteered for service at the commencement of the campaign in German East Africa, and in recognition of his past military record—having gone through the Anglo-Boer War with the Imperial Yeomanry—he was immediately selected for a commission in the 9th (Sportmen's) Battalion of the South African Infantry. His bravery in action in one of the first

Miscellaneous

severe battles, where he earned the award of the Military Cross, fully justified his selection.

While on active service he contracted the disease which subsequently caused his death, after taking up his former duties in Barkly West.

HAROLD ACTON, eldest son of the late John Adams Acton, London and Ormidale, Brodick, came to the Western front with the South Africans after the defeat of the enemy in South-West Africa, but after a spell in France he returned invalided. He was a trooper in the Jameson Raid, and was engaged in the Anglo-Boer War, as well as in other minor affairs.

Miscellaneous

HARRY TELFER, husband of Jessie Wilson, Rowan Bank, went with a Yeomanry regiment to the Eastern Mediterranean, and after serving in Gallipoli, Egypt, and Palestine, he was taken to France in June 1918, and killed there in September following.

DONALD HAY, Piper, nephew of Alexander Wooley, Invercloy, joined the London Scottish in April 1916, and served in Salonica, Egypt, Palestine, and France.

JOHN NOTMAN, a woodman employed by Messrs

Brodick-Arran and the Great War

Halliday, timber merchants, left Brodick in October 1915, and was posted to the R.F.A.

JAMES ROSS, motor driver with Kaspar Ribbeck, Invercloy, was called to the Colours on attaining military age in the spring of 1917.

LIONEL ACTON, son of the aforesaid late John Adams Acton, joined the 10th Royal Fusiliers early in the war, and served in France as a private, obtaining a commission later.

MURRAY ADAMS ACTON, brother of the above was for a time in the Army, and also in action in France.

WILLIAM HENDERSON, Sergeant, youngest son of Donald Henderson, Birchvale, Brodick, joined the American Air Force in September 1917. Trained at Aviation Camp, Waco, Texas, he is now at New York. He was previously a carpenter in Montana.

LEWIS FULLARTON, younger son of the late John Fullarton, High Glencloy, came to France with the American Flying Corps early in 1918.
He had been resident in America for many years.

THOMAS MILLAR, son of Captain Matthew Millar, Corrie, late of Corriegills, joined the American Air Force as a mechanic in the autumn of 1917, and crossed from America to France in the spring of 1918.

Names of other Arran Men on Active Service, obtained from an Official Source

Argyll and Sutherland Highlanders—

Corrie	Pte. W. Landsborough	.	Missing.
Lamlash	,, I. Bryceland	.	...
,,	,, Robt. Fairley	.	...
,,	,, John Grant	.	...
,,	,, J. M'Cubbin	.	...
,,	,, C. M'Intyre	.	...
,,	,, John M'Dowall	.	...
,,	,, W. M'Lean	.	...
,,	,, D. Saul	.	...
,,	,, J. Walker	.	...
,,	,, J. Watson	.	...
Whiting Bay	,, R. Dykes	.	...
,,	,, C. Hamilton	.	...
,,	L.-Cpl. J. M'Nicol	.	...
,,	Pte. A. M'Nicol	.	...
,,	,, A. Shaw	.	...
Southend and Kildonan	,, A. Crossley	.	...
,,	,, W. Cochrane	.	...
,,	,, A. Hamilton	.	...
,,	,, A. Miller	.	...
,,	,, W. M'Kelvie	.	...
,,	,, J. A. M'Donald	.	Killed 23/8/18.
,,	,, G. Grieve	.	...
,,	,, J. M'Bride	.	Killed 24/4/17.
,,	,, P. Nicol	.	...
,,	L.-Cpl. T. Sprowl	.	Killed 1/5/18.
,,	Pte. A. Thomson	.	...
,,	,, D. Murchie	.	...
,,	,, W. M'Donald	.	...
Shiskine	,, W. Hamilton	.	Missing 30/4/18.
,,	,, G. Stewart	.	...
,,	,, J. M'Queen	.	...
,,	,, F. G. Ritchie	.	...
,,	,, J. Brown	.	...

Brodick-Arran and the Great War

A. & S. H. (*continued*)—

Shiskine	Pte. A. Craig	...
,,	,, P. M'Crank	Awarded D.C.M. Died wds. 18/1/18.
,,	,, J. Lemon	...
,,	,, A. M'Allister	Killed 24/10/18.
,,	,, A. Purdie	...
,,	,, A. M'Hardie	...
,,	,, R. Young	...
,,	,, D. Craig	...
,,	,, A. Cochrane	...
Pirnmill	,, J. Hendry	...
Lochranza	Lieut. R. Kerr	Awarded M.C. and Belgian Croix de Guerre.
,,	Pte. D. Sutherland	...
,,	,, N. Clark	...
,,	,, D. Kerr	...

Highland Light Infantry—

Corrie	L.-Cpl. R. D. Forsyth	Killed.
,,	Pte. J. Kelso	...
,,	,, D. Watson	...
Lamlash	,, A. Allan	...
,,	,, R. Crawford	...
,,	,, A. Fullarton	...
,,	,, A. Montgomerie	...
,,	,, G. M'Gowan	Killed 1/12/17.
,,	,, N. F. Stewart	...
Whiting Bay	,, P. M'Intyre	...
Southend and Kildonan	,, N. M'Callum	...
Slidderie	L.-Cpl. A. Henderson	Killed 18/4/18.
,,	Pte. A. Spiers	...
Shiskine	,, A. M'Phee	...
,,	,, J. S. Bannatyne	...
,,	,, W. M'Laren	...
,,	,, J. Kelso	...
Pirnmill	,, G. M'Callum	...
Lochranza	Sgn. J. Kerr	...

Scottish Rifles—

Corrie	Sgt. A. Bruce	Killed.
,,	Lieut. J. C. Burns	...
Lamlash	2nd Lieut. E. Bolt	...
,,	Pte. A. Stewart	Awarded M.M.

Other Arran Men on Active Service

S.R. (*continued*)—

Lamlash	Pte. A. M'Intyre	...
Kildonan and Southend	,, J. Currie	...
Slidderie	,, J. Mullholland	...
,,	,, J. M'Dougall	...
,,	,, A. M'Allister	...
Shiskine	,, J. M'Laren	...
,,	,, J. M'Lelland	...

Royal Field Artillery—

Corrie	Gnr. D. Bruce	Killed.
,,	Dvr. J. Kerr	...
,,	Gnr. R. King	...
Lamlash	Gnr. J. Fullarton	...
,,	Sgt. A. Madden	Killed 23/5/17.
,,	Pte. A. M'Intyre	...
Whiting Bay	Bom. J. Cook	...
,,	Gnr. J. Graham	Killed.
,,	Bom. J. Hamilton	...
,,	Gnr. G. Hamilton	...
,,	Dvr. A. Hamilton	...
,,	Sgr. A. M'Kelvie	...
,,	Bom. Jas. M'Kelvie	Killed 9/4/18.
,,	,, Jack M'Kelvie	...
,,	Gnr. D. M'Intyre	...
,,	,, T. Murphy	...
,,	Staff-Sgt. A. Taylor	...
,,	Bom. J. Thomson	...
Southend and Kildonan	Pte. J. Currie	...
,,	,, D. Fox	...
,,	Dvr. J. Mathie	...
Slidderie	Sgt.-Sdlr. W. M'Allister	...
,,	Gnr. D. Stewart	...
,,	,, R. A. Spiers	...
Shiskine	Dvr. A. M'Kenzie	...
,,	Farrier John Stewart	...
,,	Lieut. H. Steel	...
,,	Dvr. J. Currie	...
,,	Sgt. W. Currie	...
Pirnmill	Dvr. M. Skillen	...
,,	,, J. Skillen	...

Cyclist Battalion—

Corrie	Pte. D. Forsyth	...

Brodick-Arran and the Great War

Royal Air Force—

Corrie	2nd A.-M. A. James .	...
,,	Pte. J. Nicol .	...
Lamlash	Flight-Sgt. I. Dempsey .	...
,,	Cadet J. Sinclair .	...
Whiting Bay .	1st A.-M. J. A. Lennox .	...
,,	Pte. A. M'Kenzie .	...
,,	3rd A.-M. W. M'Murtrie .	...
Southend and Kildonan	Pte. John Reid .	...

Seaforth Highlanders—

Corrie	Pte. J. Hastings	...
Lamlash	,, C. Allan .	...
,,	L.-Cpl. P. Allan .	...
,,	2nd Lieut. W. Buie .	...
,,	Pte. J. M'Arthur .	...
,,	,, C. M'Coll .	...
,,	,, K. M'Kay .	...
Slidderie	,, J. Mathie .	...
Shiskine	,, W. M'Phee .	...
,,	,, A. Hamilton .	...
,,	,, R. M'Gregor .	...
,,	,, R. M'Candlish .	...
,,	,, H. L. Craig .	...
,,	,, G. Buchanan .	...
Pirnmill .	,, J. Robertson .	...
Lochranza	,, A. M'Allister .	...
,,	,, J. Kerr .	...

Army Service Corps—

Corrie	Cpl. J. Keenan .	...
,,	Pte. W. Keenan .	...
,,	,, M. M'Clung .	...
,,	,, W. A. M'Millan .	...
Lamlash	,, J. Jones .	...
,,	,, N. M'Intyre .	...
,,	Capt. J. Sillars .	...
,,	Pte. G. Moore .	...
,,	,, W. Potts .	...
Whiting Bay .	,, W. Nicol .	...
Southend and Kildonan	Farrier W. Hamilton .	...
Shiskine	Pte. P. M'Kelvie .	...
,,	,, A. Baird .	...
,,	,, C. M. Weir .	...

Other Arran Men on Active Service

A.S.C. (*continued*)—
Shiskine	Pte. A. Sym	...
Lochranza	Sgt. P. A. Kerr	...
,,	Pte. A. N. Kerr	...

Royal Army Medical Corps—
Corrie	Pte. E. Kelso	...
,,	,, M. Logan	...
,,	Lieut. D. M'Dougall	
,,	Pte. E. Watson	...
Lamlash	Major C. M'Intosh	...
,,	Capt. S. D. Robertson	...
Kildonan and Southend	,, J. Downie	Awarded D.S.O. and Order of St Ann's.
Slidderie	Pte. A. Cook	...
Shiskine	Capt. C. C. Irvine	...
,,	Pte. A. M'Allister	...

Canadian Engineers—
Corrie	Sap. J. Kelso	...

Canadians—
Corrie	Pte. J. King	...
Lamlash	Major Jas. Hamilton	Awarded M.C.
,,	Pte. D. M'Lean	...
,,	Sgt. J. M'Neish	...
,,	,, R. M'Millan	Died wds. 28/10/17.
Whiting Bay	Pte. A. M'Kenzie	...
Southend and Kildonan	,, Allan Currie	...
,,	,, D. Fox	...
,,	,, J. Mathie	...
Shiskine	,, J. Currie	...
,,	Dvr. A. Robertson	...
,,	Pte. J. M'Diarmid	Died wounds 6/15.
,,	,, D. Thomson	...
Slidderie	,, A. Mullholland	Killed 9/10/16.
,,	L.-Cpl. R. Murchie	,, 4/9/17.
,,	Pte. R. M'Kechnie	,, 13/9/16.
Pirnmill	,, D. Robertson	,, in action.
Lochranza	Lieut.-Col. J. M'Millan	...

Canadian Scottish—
Lamlash	Cpl. A. Hamilton	Killed 9/11/17.

Canadian Royal Highlanders—
Whiting Bay	Cpl. J. N. S. Poole	Killed 23/4/15.

Brodick-Arran and the Great War

Black Watch—

Corrie	Piper W. King	...
Lamlash	Pte. J. Hamilton	...
,,	,, P. Keough	...
,,	,, J. Montgomerie	...
,,	,, W. Rough	...
,,	,, M. D. Sinclair	Killed 25/9/18.
Whiting Bay	,, J. Cumming	...
,,	,, J. Kirk	...
,,	,, R. M'Kelvie	Killed 25/9/17.
,,	,, R. J. M'Neil	...
,,	L.-Cpl. A. Ryrie	...
,,	Pte. N. Shaw	Killed 1/4/17.
Slidderie	,, D. M'Intyre	,, 25/3/18.
,,	,, J. Stewart	...
,,	,, C. Stewart	...
Southend and Kildonan	,, D. Cumming	Killed 28/6/17.
,,	2nd Lieut. J. B. Duncan	...
Shiskine	Pte. D. Stewart	...
,,	,, G. M'Intyre	...
,,	,, T. Watt	...
,,	,, J. Murchie	...
,,	Sgt. N. Henderson	Killed 3/9/16.
,,	Pte. P. Neil	...
,,	,, P. Bannatyne	...
,,	,, N. Finnegan	...
,,	,, A. Craig	...
,,	,, W. King	...
,,	,, W. Wilson	...
Pirnmill	,, R. Henderson	...
,,	Sgt.-Maj. J. Henderson	Twice mentioned in despatches; awarded Belgian Croix de Guerre.
,,	Pte. R. Robertson	Awarded French Croix de Guerre.
,,	,, J. Craig	Killed 25/9/15.
,,	Sgt. P. Craig	Awarded D.C.M. and M.M.
,,	Pte. M. Gardiner	...
,,	,, R. Robertson	Killed 25/9/15.
Lochranza	,, H. Orr	...

Other Arran Men on Active Service

Royal Garrison Artillery—

Corrie	Gnr. R. Logan	...
Lamlash	,, W. R. Briggs	...
,,	Bom. R. S. M'Neish	...
,,	Cpl. W. Stevenson	...
,,	Gnr. D. Stewart	...
,,	,, J. A. C. Sharp	...
,,	Sgn. G. Allan	...
Whiting Bay	Gnr. J. Auld	...
,,	,, J. Hyslop	...
,,	,, P. M'Kenzie	...
,,	,, J. Buie	...
Southend and Kildonan	,, G. Cook	...
Slidderie	,, J. B. Murchie	...
,,	Bom. D. M'Allister	...
,,	Gnr. C. M'Kelvie	...
Shiskine	Pte. J. Sinclair	...
,,	,, J. Stewart	...
,,	Gnr. N. M'Bride	...
,,	,, J. Currie	...
,,	,, D. M'Leod	...
,,	Cpl. C. Henderson	...
,,	Gnr. M. Matheson	...
Pirnmill	,, A. Kelso	...
Lochranza	Lieut. J. Kerr	...
,,	Gnr. R. Kelso	...
,,	Cpl. I. M'Millan	...
,,	Gnr. A. Watson	...

Cameron Highlanders—

Corrie	Pte. A. M'Lauchlan	...
Lamlash	L.-Cpl. C. Burke	...
,,	Cpl. J. Buie	...
,,	Pte. H. Buie	...
,,	,, A. Kelso	Killed 4/4/16.
,,	L.-Cpl. A. Kerr	...
,,	Pte. M. Kerr	...
,,	Sgt. A. Montgomery	...
,,	Cpl. A. M'Innes	...
,,	Pte. A. M'Lean	...
,,	,, J. Walker	Died 11/12/15.
Whiting Bay	Cpl. Jas. M'Murtrie	Killed 27/6/16.
,,	,, John M'Murtrie	...

Brodick-Arran and the Great War.

Gordon Highlanders—
Corrie	Pte. A. M'Killop	...
Lamlash	,, R. Jones	...
Whiting Bay	,, C. Bannatyne	...
,,	,, P. Downie	...
Southend and Kildonan	L.-Cpl. John Reid	...
Shiskine	,, A. Watson	Killed 17/5/17.
,,	Pte. D. Reside	...

Machine Gun Corps—
Corrie	Pte. A. C. M'Dougall	...
Lamlash	,, J. Hyslop	...
,,	,, G. M'Intyre	...
,,	,, C. Stirling	Awarded M.M.
Whiting Bay	,, R. Allison	...
Southend and Kildonan	L.-Cpl. R. Lindsay	...
Slidderie	Pte. J. Ferguson	...
Lochranza	Gnr. R. M'Millan	...

North Staffordshires—
Corrie	L.-Cpl. J. Reid	...

Royal Engineers—
Corrie	L.-Cpl. J. Tierney	...
Lamlash	Spr. W. Fingland	...
,,	Pte. Wm. Lang	...
,,	Spr. D. Middleton	...
,,	Cpl. J. M'Millan	...
,,	Sgt. A. Thomson	...
Whiting Bay	Spr. A. K. Kerr	Killed 2/6/18.
,,	,, R. N. Kilpatrick	...
,,	,, D. Thomson	...
Southend and Kildonan	2nd Lieut. A. M'Neil	...
Shiskine	Spr. A. M'Kenzie	...
,,	,, D. M'Kenzie	...
,,	Capt. A. M'Allister	...
,,	Spr. G. Bannatyne	...
Pirnmill	,, J. Anderson	...
Lochranza	,, D. Sutherland	...
,,	,, Dugald Kerr	...
,,	Lieut. M. D. Kerr	...

United States Air Force—
Corrie	2nd A.-M. T. Millar	...

Other Arran Men on Active Service

United States Army (Infantry)—
Whiting Bay	Sgt.-Major A. Kennedy	...
Pirnmill	Pte. N. Robertson	...
Lochranza	,, J. Watson	...

Labour Battalion—
Lamlash	Pte. P. Murphy	...
Whiting Bay	,, W. Evans	...
,,	,, D. Murray	...
Southend and Kildonan	,, J. Cook	...

Lovat Scouts—
Southend and Kildonan	Cpl. D. Lindsay	...
Shiskine	Pte. J. M'Diarmid	...
Lochranza	,, D. Kerr	...

Royal Scots Fusiliers—
Lamlash	Pte. W. Murray	...
,,	Lieut. J. B. Sweet	...
,,	Pte. J. Saul	Killed 11/2/15.
,,	,, W. Saul	...
Whiting Bay	,, J. Boa	...
,,	,, J. Bell	...
,,	,, E. Erwin	...
,,	,, J. Kerr	...
,,	Cpl. D. M'Intyre	...
,,	Pte. J. M'Giffen	...
,,	,, T. Paisley	...
,,	,, R. Wishart	Killed 2/8/17.
Slidderie	L.-Cpl. H. Wilson	...
Southend and Kildonan	Pte. J. Forest	Killed 25/9/17.
,,	,, Stewart Storie	,, 12/10/15.
,,	,, Samuel Storie	...
,,	,, W. Shaw	...
,,	,, A. Thomson	...
Shiskine	,, W. Lang	...
,,	,, D. M'Kenzie	...
,,	,, J. Sinclair	...
,,	L.-Cpl. A. M'Kenzie	...
Lochranza	Pte. A. Kerr	...

Brodick-Arran and the Great War

Argyll and Bute Mounted Battery—

Southend and Kildonan	Pte. J. Miller	...
,,	,, J. M'Donald	...
Pirnmill	,, J. Kerr	...

Tank Corps—

Southend and Kildonan	Gnr. John Reid	...

King's Own Scottish Borderers—

Lamlash	Pte. J. Campbell	Killed 24/4/17.
,,	,, J. Gordon	...
,,	Lieut. R. Hamilton	...
Southend and Kildonan	Pte. G. Forest	...
Shiskine	,, A. Currie	Missing, presumed killed 4/9/17.
,,	,, R. Marshall	...
,,	Cpl. W. Robertson	...
Pirnmill	L.-Cpl. J. M'Cormack	Killed.
,,	Pte. Jas. Thomson	,,
,,	,, C. Robertson	...
Lochranza	,, A. M'Allister	Wnd. in France, died 16/6/18.

Scottish Horse—

Southend and Kildonan	Pte. W. Fraser	Died May 1917.

Australian Forces—

Lamlash	Pte. J. M'Lean	Missing since landing Gallipoli.
Southend and Kildonan	Pte. D. M'Kinnon	...
...	William Cumming	...

Australian Field Artillery—

Lamlash	Dvr. W. A. Inglis	...

Australian Light Horse—

Lamlash	Sgt. J. Inglis Sweet	...
Shiskine	Lieut. A. Currie	Awarded Military Medal. Killed.

Royal Scots—

Lamlash	Pte. P. Boa	...
,,	,, J. F. Campbell	Killed.

Other Arran Men on Active Service

Royal Scots (*continued*)—
Lamlash	Pte. R. M'Kenzie	...
,,	,, P. Trow	...
Whiting Bay	,, R. Elliot	...
Slidderie	,, W. Mathie	...
Shiskine	,, J. Anderson	...
Pirnmill	,, J. M'Bride	...

Royal Fusiliers—
Lamlash . Pte. W. M'Gowan . . ...

Army Veterinary Corps—
Lamlash	Sgt. A. Hamilton	...
,,	Q.M. Sgt. J. S. Currie	...
Whiting Bay	B.E.A. Major W. Kennedy	Awarded D.S.O.
Shiskine	Pte. J. Hamilton	...
,,	,, J. C. M'Lauchlan	...

New Zealand Forces—
Lamlash	Sgt. J. Allan	Killed 2/5/15.
Whiting Bay	Pte. J. Hamilton	,, 25/9/16.
,,	Sgt. W. Hamilton	...
Southend and Kildonan	Pte. J. M'Kinnon	Killed 15/9/16.
,,	,, A. M'Kinnon	...
Slidderie	,, J. H. Henderson	...
,,	,, P. M'Allister	Killed 12/10/17.
,,	Dvr. J. Stewart	...
Shiskine	Pte. W. M'Allister	...
Lochranza	L.-Cpl. J. Kerr	...

South African Forces—
Lamlash . Pte. J. Hamilton . . ...

Anzac Cyclist Battalion—
Lamlash . Sgn. W. Watson . . ...

Water Transport Corps—
Lamlash . Cpl. J. Hunter . . ...

2nd Wiltshires—
Lamlash . Lieut. M. Sillars . . Awarded M.C.

Inland Water Transport—
Lamlash . Lieut. N. Sillars . . ...
Whiting Bay . ,, D. M'Kenzie . . ...

Indian Medical Service—
Lamlash . Capt. R. Sweet . . Awarded D.S.O.

Brodick-Arran and the Great War

Scots Guards—
Lamlash . Pte. J. Shiels . . . Died on service, Feb. 1917.
Shiskine . ,, A. M'Queen . . ...
Pirnmill . ,, A. Murchie . . ...

Northumberland Fusiliers—
Lamlash . Pte. J. Stirling . . . ...

South Wales Borderers—
Whiting Bay . Cpl. J. M. Gray . . ...

Glasgow Yeomanry—
Whiting Bay . Sgt. H. Hamilton . . ...

Royal Horse Artillery—
Whiting Bay . Gnr. R. Kerr . . . ...

Manchester Rifles—
Whiting Bay . 2nd Lt. D. N. M'Murtrie . ...

Army Service Corps (Motor Transport)—
Southend and Pte. A. Cook . . . ...
Kildonan . ...
,, . ,, A. Hunter . . . ...
,, . ,, P. Hamilton . . ...
Slidderie . ,, R. H. Spiers . . ...

Border Regiment—
Southend and Cpl. R. Campbell . . ...
Kildonan .

Rifle Brigade—
Southend and L.-Cpl. P. M'Donald . Awarded M.M.
Kildonan

Scots Greys—
Southend and Cpl. J. Sprowl . . . ...
Kildonan

Lothian and Border Horse—
Southend and Pte. Chas. Wescott . . ...
Kildonan

Officer Cadet Battalion—
Slidderie . Cadet P. H. M'Kelvie . ...

London Scottish—
Shiskine . Pte. J. M'Master . . ...

Royal Inniskilling Fusiliers—
Shiskine . Pte. J. Brown . . . ...

Other Arran Men on Active Service

King's Royal Rifles—
Shiskine . Pte. D. Bannatyne . . ...

Royal Flying Corps—
Shiskine . Lieut. W. Armit . . ...

Royal Marine Artillery—
Lochranza . Gnr. D. Brown . . . ...

Chaplains—
Whiting Bay . Capt. Rev. J. D. Brown . ...
Southend and ,, Rev. D. Conachar . ...
Kildonan .
Shiskine . ,, Rev. W. M'Leod . ...

Royal Navy—
Corrie . . A.S. A. Kelso . . . ...
,, . . Sgn. A. Kerr . . . ...
,, . . O.S. J. Lamb . . . ...
,, . . ,, C. Russell . . . ...
,, . . Engr. T. Simpson . . ...
,, . . O.S. A. Watson . . ...
Lamlash . L.S. J. A. Crawford . . ...
,, . . C.P.O. R. Dempsey . . Mentioned in Despatches.
,, . . A.B. W. G. Dempsey . Awarded D.S.M.
Whiting Bay . O.S. A. W. C. Watt . . ...
,, . A.B. J. M'Intosh . . ...
,, . E.R.A. D. M'Nicol . . ...
Southend and Chief Engr. W. Cook . ...
Kildonan . ...
,, . A.B. W. Forest . . . ...
Slidderie . ,, W. Henderson . . ...

Royal Naval Reserve—
Lamlash . Lieut. A. Crawford . . Lost at sea.
,, . . A.B. J. Crawford . . ...
,, . . O.S. T. Dempsey . . ...
,, . . Sgn. J. Hamilton . . ...
,, . . O.S. P. Kelso . . . ...
,, . . Engr.-Lieut. J. M'Coll . ...
,, . . Engr. J. M'Intyre . . ...
,, . . Lieut. D. M'Kelvie . . ...
,, . . Stoker D. M'Dowall . . ...
,, . . Engr.-Lieut. D. M'Nicol . ...
Whiting Bay . ,, A. R. Nicol . ...
Slidderie . Lieut. D. M'Allister . . ...
,, . W.O.Engr. H. M'Allister . ...

Brodick-Arran and the Great War

R.N.R. (*continued*)—

Slidderie	3rd Engr. J. Stewart.	...
Shiskine	Seaman J. Hamilton	...
,,	Lieut.-Com. J. Nairn	...
,,	,, J. Weir.	...
,,	Seaman W. Arthur.	...
Pirnmill.	Stoker J. Kelso.	...
,,	Seaman H. Thomson	...
,,	,, W. Kerr	...
Lochranza	Lieut. J. K. M'Millan	...
,,	Stoker F. Kerr.	...
,,	Seaman J. Kerr	...

Royal Naval Volunteer Reserve—

Lamlash	Lieut. W. Black	...
,,	O.S. Michael Cannon	...
Whiting Bay.	W.O. A. Cook.	...
,,	Gnr. D. R. Shaw	...
,,	,, J. Thomson	Died at sea, 24/11/17.
Shiskine	Seaman N. Delargey	...
Pirnmill.	Seaman-Gnr. C. Craig	...
,,	Seaman L. M'Bride.	...
,,	Seaman-Gnr. J. Currie	...
Lochranza	Artificer A. Miller	...

Royal Naval Division—

Slidderie	L.S. G. S. Kinner	...
,,	A.B. F. Wilson.	...
Shiskine	Pte. G. Whitelaw	...
,,	,, F. Wilson.	...
,,	,, R. Purdie.	...

Coastal Motor Boat, Royal Navy—

Whiting Bay.	C.M.M. D. Kennedy	...

Motor Boat Ambulance—

Whiting Bay.	Engr. G. Hamilton.	...

Printed in Great Britain
by Amazon